Praise for *Cat Calls*

"engaging and entertaining"

"When it comes to felines, Jeanne Adlon is a real expert. . . . In *Cat Calls*, her engaging and entertaining anecdotes are perfectly blended with solid, practical advice for cat owners. There's a chapter on eating, a chapter on chubby cats, a chapter on diva cats who demand the star treatment—hey, wait a minute! I think this book is about Garfield!"

Jim Davis
Creator of *Garfield*

"a must-read"

"Jeanne Adlon's extraordinary life as a cat sitter is a must-read for any cat lover. Her wonderful stories of the many cats she has cared for will touch your heart, while her commonsense advice is priceless."

Dr. Marty Becker, DVM
Resident veterinarian for *Good Morning America*, *The Dr. Oz Show*, and *Parade* magazine
Coauthor of *Chicken Soup for the Pet Lover's Soul*

"a tasty smorgasbord of fun"

"Calling All Cat Lovers! Cat expert and cat sitter Jeanne Adlon, with purr-fessional writer Susan Logan, bring readers a tasty smorgasbord of fun kitty anecdotes seasoned with sound advice and lots of furry inspiration. Paws-itively delightful!"

Amy D. Shojai, Certified Animal Behavior Consultant
Author of numerous pet-care books and Founder of Cat Writers' Association

"entertaining ... fascinating"

"Jeanne Adlon and Susan Logan have been giving top billing to cats for years now. Cats are clearly fascinating and mysterious, but what makes *Cat Calls* so entertaining are some of the fascinating things that happen when people share their homes with felines. Woven through the LOL anecdotes is good information about cat care and welfare. Even experienced cat lovers might learn—I did."

Steve Dale, Certified Behavior Consultant
Author of "My Pet World" and Host of *Steve Dale's Pet World*
Contributing Editor, *USA Weekend*

"a delightful page-turner"

"Cats on Broadway and every street in New York City are fortunate felines thanks to the pet-sitting savvy of Jeanne Adlon. With the aid of *Cat Fancy* editor Susan Logan, Jeanne has crafted a delightful page-turner about cats living in the Big Apple. This collection of feline tales puts the WOW in Me-WOW!"

Arden Moore
Host of *Oh Behave!* and Founder of www.fourleggedlife.com

"I savored every word"

"Jeanne Adlon, New York City's most famous cat sitter, dishes on some of her hilarious feline charges and their quirky owners with liberal helpings of good advice flavored by *Cat Fancy* editor Susan Logan. I savored every word!"

Sandy Robins
Author of *Fabulous Felines*

"great job"

"Every cat book should be entertaining and educational. This book is certainly both. Great job."

Dusty Rainbolt
Author of *Cat Wrangling Made Easy*

Cat Calls

WONDERFUL STORIES AND PRACTICAL ADVICE FROM A VETERAN CAT SITTER

Cat Calls

WONDERFUL STORIES AND PRACTICAL ADVICE FROM A VETERAN CAT SITTER

Jeanne Adlon • Susan Logan

FOREWORD BY JIM DAVIS, CREATOR OF *GARFIELD*

SQUAREONE
PUBLISHERS

The advice in this book is based on the personal experiences and research of the authors. It is not intended as a substitute for consulting with a qualified veterinarian or feline behaviorist. The publisher and authors are not responsible for any adverse effects or consequences resulting from the use of any of the suggestions discussed in this book. All matters pertaining to your cat's physical health should be supervised by a health care professional.

A portion of the royalties of this book is being donated to animal rescue, rehabilitation, and preservation organizations.

Cover Designer: Jeannie Tudor
Interior Illustrations: Cathy Morrison
Typesetter: Gary A. Rosenberg
Project Manager: Karen Jones
In-House Editor: Joanne Abrams
Front Cover Photo: Getty Images, Inc.
Back Cover Photos: Karen Jones (for Jeanne
   Adlon) and Amy Hooper (for Susan Logan)

Square One Publishers
115 Herricks Road
Garden City Park, NY 11040
(516) 535-2010 • (877) 900-BOOK

ISBN 978-0-7570-0344-8

Contents

*This is dedicated to all the wonderful caring people
in the world who help animals in need.*
                                                    –J.A.

*I wish to dedicate this book to Gulliver, Chamois, Chloe,
Sophie and Madison. I can think of no finer friends or companions.*
                                                    –S.L.

Foreword

BY JIM DAVIS
CREATOR OF *GARFIELD*

I like to think I know a little something about cats. I grew up on a farm in Indiana with twenty-five barn cats and in 1978 created an overweight orange tabby with a penchant for lasagna. (Hint: his namesake is America's twentieth president.)

But when it comes to felines, Jeanne Adlon is a real expert. As a cat sitter in New York City for more than thirty-five years, Jeanne has cared for hundreds of kitties in everything from one-room walk-ups to deluxe penthouses. And it's obvious that her work is a true labor of love.

And the stories! How about the cat who tried to gobble up a twenty-pound turkey on Thanksgiving? Or the cats whose owner insisted they dine on kosher cold cuts for Passover? Or the kitty who shared his apartment with a huge tarantula?

Jeanne's engaging and entertaining anecdotes are perfectly blended with solid, practical advice for cat owners. There are stories about eating, chubby cats, and diva cats who demand the star treatment—hey, wait a minute! I think this book is about Garfield!

Before I forget, I want to mention Susan Logan, the inimitable editor of *Cat Fancy* magazine. We've had the pleasure of working with Sue and *Cat Fancy* for a few years, and they've graciously allowed Garfield to weigh in on everything from catnip to cloning in his monthly column.

One thing I've learned from my many years drawing Garfield: people are passionate about their pets. It's wonderful to find people like Jeanne and Susan who share this passion.

Enjoy!

Acknowledgments

Jeanne Adlon wishes to thank . . .

I have many people to thank for helping me through the process of writing this book. First of all, I could not have even begun to put this all down on paper without my wonderful co-writer, Susan Logan, editor of *Cat Fancy* magazine. Her patience, guidance, and good humor have made this project a delight. Thank you, Susan! I also want to thank all the wonderful and supportive people at www.CatChannel.com, where I write my weekly Cat Expert column.

I want to thank Karen Jones, the project manager of *Cat Calls*, who convinced me I had a story to tell in the first place. Now a friend, she steered this project through the years of development while standing firm in her belief that *Cat Calls* was a great book. It would never have happened without her.

I was thrilled by all the people who have read the book and given it such wonderful praise such as Jim Davis, creator of *Garfield*, Dr. Marty Becker, Amy Shojai, Sandy Robins, Steve Dale, Dusty Rainbolt, and Arden Moore. Thank you all for your support.

I want to thank my publisher, Rudy Shur, for his support and belief in this book, and my editor, Joanne Abrams, a true cat person, for her insight and dedication. I also want to thank Cathy Morrison for her wonderful illustrations.

There is also my dear friend, Mary Anderson, whose warmth, courage, and strength inspire me and everyone who knows her. Alice, aka "Mamie" Glasberg, is always filled with love and encouragement, and like a second mom to me. Lois and Ray Shanfeld were the first customers of my cat store, Cat Cottage, in the 1970s, and are supportive friends to this day. I am also grateful to my brother, George, and sister-in-law, Karen, who truly know the meaning of love and compassion for our furry friends, and to wonderful Sue Southard, a true friend. Thanks also to sweet Helen Coutts, Jerry L. Style, and Sally Reed.

I want to thank the hundreds of cats that I have cared for, and all my clients, past and present. Without them, there would be no *Cat Calls* to share with you. Last, but not least, I am grateful to the wonderful cats I live with and to Ziggy, the little dog who fits into our feline family perfectly.

Susan Logan wishes to thank . . .

I'm compelled to thank God for every opportunity I've ever had. For whatever reason, He gave me a platform to be an advocate for His magnificent creatures: cats.

I want to thank Jeanne Adlon for sharing her stories with me. A true original, who is quick to laugh at herself, Jeanne is as delightful and fun in person as her stories are to read. She is also one of the most genuine, kind, and altruistic people I've ever known.

When I first got the phone call from Karen Jones, who invited me to co-author this book, naturally, I was excited about the opportunity. Karen's skills as a writer, manager, and gentle nudger kept me on track and made the creative process much easier than it could have been.

I thank my parents, Walter and Lona Bumbulis, for instilling in me compassion and reverence for all God's creatures, from the tiniest honeybee to the behemoth blue whale.

My dear sister, Karen, entrusted me with the care of her cat while she went to summer camp, and Gulliver became my first feline friend. While she was away, Gulliver got hit by a car. When my mom picked him up, I could see he was still breathing so I ran to my room and prayed for him, and he miraculously recovered. That was my first act of feline advocacy.

My former sister-in-law, Kathy Scott, was the first cat rescuer I'd ever known. She found two adult cats who needed homes, and I agreed to take them in. Chamois and Chloe, in turn, gave me a career path I could never have anticipated, for it was their presence in my life and my experience as an editor that opened the opportunity to become *Cat Fancy's* editor at parent publisher BowTie, Inc. Chamois and Chloe lived with me for more than thirteen years and got me through some of the greatest losses of my life. They showed me what wonderful, loyal friends cats are and taught me the value of just showing up for someone in need.

I want to acknowledge Rudy Shur for publishing this book and assembling a thoughtful, talented team at Square One: editor Joanne Abrams, who massaged the text while maintaining its unique tone and voice; and Cathy Morrison, whose illustrations captured with such warmth cats' lovable antics.

I'm privileged to work in the cat writing profession, in which there are no competitors, only fellow feline advocates. Steve Dale, Arden Moore, Amy Shojai, Dusty Rainbolt, Sandy Robins, and Dr. Marty Becker are all friends and mentors whose encouragement inspires me to give back to the entire cat writing community. And the man behind *Garfield*, Jim Davis, is beyond delightful to work with.

My cats, Madison and Sophie, sat beside me as I added the final touches to this book. Everyone should be so lucky to be between two purring cats! For them and all felines, I will be forever grateful.

A Word About Gender

Your cat is just as likely to be a girl as a boy, or you may have a family of cats, male and female. Because we want to give equal acknowledgment to both genders—and because we don't want to refer to any cat as an "it"—throughout this book, we have tried to alternate the use of male and female pronouns such as *he* and *she, his* and *her.* Although not as adorable as cats, veterinarians are important, too, so we have also alternated the use of male and female pronouns when referring to our kitties' doctors.

Cat Calls

How I Got Into This Kooky Business

Cat Calls is my story of over thirty-five amazing years as a cat sitter in the "city that never sleeps." It's been quite a journey, filled with hundreds of fascinating felines—each with a tale to tell. I am happy to share my stories with you and, along the way, provide some sound, practical advice for cat lovers everywhere.

I am often asked what it is like being a full-time cat sitter, entering people's homes all over Manhattan to care for beloved felines while their owners are away. I usually say, "I love my job and it's *never* dull." Let me assure you this profession is not for wimps. I have been called upon to scramble up high-rise fire escapes, break into apartments, dodge tarantulas, feed pampered kitties in Waterford goblets, help correct some pretty bizarre behaviors—both feline and human—and cope with the unexpected.

I remember a sweltering summer day during a massive blackout that crippled most of the East Coast. I had a cat-sitting house call in a high-rise building, and somehow, I had to get there.

Waiting for me was Sabrina, the thirteen-year-old gray and white cat for whom I was caring. She was frail due to kidney problems, and in the intense heat with no air conditioning, I was very worried that she would not have enough fresh water to drink.

I have claustrophobia, so with the building elevator not working, I asked the doorman if he could loan me a flashlight. Armed with his small penlight and weighed down with my usual backpack filled with treats and toys, I gingerly climbed the emergency stairs in pitch blackness trying to find the tenth floor.

Praying I would not break my neck, I steadied my nerves by trying to imagine myself walking along a sunny beach so my claustrophobia would not get the best of me. I finally found my way to the right floor, opened the apartment door, and there was lovely little Sabrina, waiting for me.

"Sabrina," I said, "you have no idea what I went through to get to you today!" She stared back at me in that self-assured feline fashion and, with a tilt of her head, indicated that I should hurry up with the food. Cats always know the bottom line.

Exhausted, I remember thinking, "How did I ever get into this kooky cat-sitting business?"

Cleveland Amory and Me

I grew up on Ninety-sixth Street and Columbus Avenue in the Upper West Side of New York City. We lived in a wonderful old brownstone. One day when I was nine years old, I found a tiny kitten crying on the stoop. I remember quickly running upstairs to fetch a cardboard box, a small blanket, and some food. I was going to rescue this kitty and make sure she was okay. Well, when I got back outside, my heart sank. The kitten was gone. I hoped her mom found her and brought her back to wherever the little family called home, but I have never forgotten that experience. I think I knew from that day on that cats would play a part in my life, and it has certainly been true.

After I graduated from the School of Art and Design in New York City, I landed a job at a trendy fashion boutique called Fancy That on Seventy-second Street and Lexington Avenue. My mother worked in the fashion industry, so I had it in my blood.

One day, Cleveland Amory walked into the store with his wife. At the time, he was a popular reviewer for *TV Guide* and later became even more famous for his best-selling books *The Cat Who Came for Christmas, The Cat and the Curmudgeon,* and *The Best Cat Ever.* I told him how much I admired his Fund for Animals rescue work. He said, "We could use volunteers," so I signed up.

Six months later, Cleveland offered me a job. I even cared for his beloved Polar Bear, the cat he rescued and made famous in his books. In fact, I am mentioned in *The Cat Who Came for Christmas*. Polar Bear was a very shy kitty. He liked to be petted, but I got the feeling he could take it or leave it unless Cleveland was petting him. Their bond was deep.

Cleveland was an outspoken man with lots of wild hair to match his flamboyant personality. He once came back from California with a rescued kitten he'd smuggled onto the plane. Apparently, because he was so large, no one noticed that he had the kitten safely secured inside his jacket. Those certainly were different days! We all were very upset with him, and he then had the gall to say, "Who wants this kitten?" You guessed it. I ended up taking her and named her Bananas because I thought that what he'd done was bananas.

I had a nice garden apartment at the time, but once, I feared I'd lost the cat. I ran outside yelling across the fence, "Bananas! Bananas!" The neighbors probably thought I was bananas. It turned out she was inside the apartment the whole time. I was very lucky; I had Bananas for twenty years and she never was sick a day in her life. Old age just crept up on her. She passed away peacefully right at home.

Although the Fund for Animals did a lot of good for animals, it was a tough job for me. The stories of cruelty and abandonment were very painful. One day when I picked up a file, an assistant flew across the office and ripped it from my hands. "You don't want to look at this, Jeanne," she said, and she was right. There are things I would rather not know.

A friend then told me, "Jeanne, you either have to learn to deal with it, or you have to get out of this job." I knew he was right.

John Lennon and *Cats*

I left the Fund for Animals and on November 1, 1974, I opened The Cat Cottage, a gift shop for cats and cat lovers where I also boarded customers' cats.

Although I custom designed two-story wooden cages for my charges, I ended up giving the kitties full run of the store. I made my own cat toys, which I sold along with treats, stationery, and kitty-themed gifts. I did very little advertising, but word spread throughout Manhattan because having a store exclusively for and about cats was unique at the time.

One day, I looked out the window to see a big stretch limo pull up. Out ran John Lennon! He flew up the stairs. Apparently, he had seen the cat tree in the window display, because he went straight for it. It was full of cat hair because my furry boarders were always climbing all over it, but that's the one he wanted.

As quickly as he came in, he dragged the cat tree out of the corner and, in doing so, got cat hair all over his dark clothes. I apologized for the cat hair and he said, "Not a problem." He put his cash on the counter and dashed out. "Keep the change," he said, so I did.

Lennon came to the store with his wife Yoko Ono and son Sean several times. Each time they dropped by, they would draw a large crowd. I had always loved Lennon's music, but who knew he was a cat lover as well?

Once, a striking young woman who looked like a dancer or a ballerina asked if she could observe the cats in my store. She said she was going to be appearing in a new Broadway show called *Cats.*

I chuckled a little and said, "Sure, be my guest." I thought she was nuts. She just walked around and watched the cats, who gave her plenty to watch, believe me.

At the time, nobody knew that this would be such a big Broadway show. I went to see *Cats* several times and loved it all—the music, the costumes, the makeup, everything.

A Cat Sitter Is Born

One fateful day, a long-time customer asked me if I would be willing to go to her house to watch her cat because she no longer wanted to board him at my store. I said to myself, "Wow! What an interesting idea!" That was the very first cat call I ever made, and the rest, as they say, is history.

The cat's name was Marcel Marceau. When I boarded him in my store, he was very aggressive and territorial, but in his own home, he was a real mush. It made me realize that cats are really better off in their own territory, and that going to them was best, even if it meant traveling from the East River to the Hudson River. I named my new traveling business Cat Calls.

I put Cat Calls on my business card and encouraged clients to pass the word—and they did. Little by little, my new cat-sitting business started to grow. People knew I was a real cat lover, and they could trust me in their homes.

Back to the Future

I have some amazing cat tales to tell! This book presents true accounts of what I have gone through to care for the kitties entrusted to me. As you will see, I take that trust seriously—to an extreme, in some cases—and always with a deep sense of love and commitment. I once trekked through a blinding blizzard on Christmas Day with a stress fracture and heel spur to make a house call. My foot was in a cast and I hobbled along with a cane. As I sank down into each snow drift, I laughed at myself. Sometimes, it's all you can do, and I know that's what kept me going. I was thinking I must take care of the kitties, just like the U.S. Postal Service, whether rain or sleet or snow, I must deliver the TLC—and I do.

I have continually been asked for advice on all kinds of cat care, both by my clients and by the weekly readers of my column found on www.CatChannel.com. It's all here to help you live a better life with your kitties, so please enjoy. This book is for all the wonderful cats out there and the people who love them!

Adopting 101

I have always been an animal lover, and by caring for people's cats as a full-time cat sitter for over thirty-five years, I have seen how truly special the human/feline bond can be. That said, adopting a cat can bring much joy and unconditional love into your life. Cats are wonderful companions and easy to care for. They do not require constant attention or fuss. In fact, most of the time they prefer doing their own thing.

You just never know when the opportunity to adopt a kitty will come your way. As I always say, when opportunity knocks, you should open the door. Sometimes, though, people need a little nudge in the right direction.

Not too long ago, I received a phone call from a family that needed to find a home for a wonderful cat whom they had named Jeter, after the Yankee ball player. Because of my work as a cat sitter, I often get these calls, and I do my best to help. Immediately, I thought of one of my favorite clients, Tucker, her husband, Brian, and their daughter, Lilia. They had lost their kitty about six months earlier. When I called Tucker, she thanked me for the offer but said that her family was not yet ready for a new cat. But something told me I should not leave it at that. When you have worked with cats and their owners as long as I have, you get a sense that some things are meant to be. So with some gentle persuasion, I convinced Tucker's family to just meet Jeter.

On the ride to Jeter's home, the family made it clear that they would see Jeter, but they were absolutely *not* going to take him. Well, Jeter had other ideas. The minute we arrived, the cat ran right over to Brian, Tucker, and Lilia and took turns sitting on their laps. Within five minutes, the family asked if they could borrow a carrier to take Jeter home.

Since that day, Jeter has become a much-loved member of the family. In fact, Tucker called me recently to thank me again for bringing them together. Nothing gives me greater joy than finding good homes for kitties.

You, too, can give a cat a wonderful home. Other then the desire to bring a cat into your life and the willingness to provide the necessities along with loving care, adopting a cat is relatively easy. This chapter presents some commonsense suggestions to get you started and guides you in introducing your new family member to your household.

ADOPTING A CAT

You probably know that there are lots of places where you can find cats for adoption. As you may have already guessed, my top recommendation is that you choose a shelter, where you'll find plenty of kitties who need good homes.

If you adopt from a shelter, you can be assured your cat will have been examined and treated by a vet. This includes looking for fleas, worms, and ear mites; spaying and neutering, if the cat is old enough; microchipping; and testing for feline leukemia and other diseases. A private adoption may not bring that assurance.

One of my clients adopted two sweet kittens, Lance and Lexi, with whom the family fell in love immediately. However, they adopted from a private home, and only after the first visit to the vet did they discover that both cats had feline leukemia. This weakens the immune system and makes cats vulnerable to all kinds of illnesses. Since the family could not bear to give up Lance and Lexi, they followed a regimen of required care. One kitty has since passed away, but the other is still here, happy, active, and deeply loved. If you adopt from a private home or rescue group, take your new cat to the vet within a few days so that you will know his health status and be able to provide the best care possible.

There may also be a neighborhood stray you have noticed and are curious about. Sadly, many strays are actually abandoned cats. If you are able to get close enough to feed or touch one without her running away, she probably had a home once and was discarded or became lost because she had no ID tag. If the cat lets you approach, consider giving her a new loving family.

If you adopt your cat from a shelter, you can be assured that he has been examined and treated by a vet. Most important, you will be helping out a wonderful kitty in need of a home.

Two cats can keep
each other company
when you're away
from home. This
usually results in
happier kitties who
are less likely to
become bored and
get into mischief.

Please know that very often, a cat chooses you. Visit your local shelters and see which kitties work their way into your heart and home. Before you get there, though, be sure to consider two important questions: Would it be better to get two cats than one, and do you want a kitten or an older cat?

Two Cats Can Be Better Than One

If you can afford it, I suggest adopting two cats at the same time because it is hard to introduce a second one into the home at a later time. Two cats can keep each other company, and you won't have to feel guilty when leaving them to go to work. Also, there is no better entertainment than watching them race around and play with each other. I believe that two cats tend to be less destructive in the home than one bored, single cat. As I often say, boredom can lead to mischief. Surprisingly enough, two cats are not much more work than one.

Kittens or Cats?

There is a great need to adopt older cats. Some of these cats were greatly beloved by owners who, for one reason or another, could not continue to care for them. These cats are often sweet and affectionate and have settled down, so you no longer have to deal with the boundless energy of youth. I often say that older cats and senior people make great housemates.

Kittens are adorable, of course, but are much more rambunctious and far more work. You will have to watch

Cagney and Lacey in the Deep Freeze

I once had to care for two cute kitties, Cagney and Lacey, during one of the coldest winters on record. When I first entered the small apartment, I was hit by a blast of freezing air. The outdoor terrace door had been left open by mistake. I was horrified and quickly started a search for the poor cats. Finally, I found two very cold, very scared kitties huddled together in a closet. They were lucky. They might have fallen off the terrace during a strong blast of winter wind. Once the apartment warmed up, I gave them some very well-deserved treats. My client was stunned when I told him, but it was a good thing he thought to have a cat sitter in.

them carefully, and their high energy levels and playfulness can sometimes get them into trouble. Also be aware that within a few months, kittens should be neutered to avoid unwanted births and help prevent behavioral and medical problems. This need not be a financial burden; there are low-cost spay and neuter clinics, and if you need to find homes for a litter of kittens, rescue groups can help. Believe me, it pays to get your cat neutered at the time recommended by your veterinarian. A friend waited too long to get his female kitten spayed, and when she went into her first heat, she literally howled at the moon and would leap onto the front door knob, swinging back and forth in a desperate attempt to get out of the house. Her howling and distress were so constant that he had to resort to keeping her in his garage at night (with the essentials of food, water, and litter) just to get some sleep. She was taken to the vet as soon as possible.

While kittens are fun, these bundles of energy aren't right for everyone. Older cats, who have already settled down, make great pets, especially for seniors.

DISTINCTIVE FELINE
POLAR BEAR—A STAR IS BORN

Immortalized by his owner, Cleveland Amory, in *The Cat Who Came for Christmas* and other bestsellers, Polar Bear was one lucky cat. Having risen from a scrappy stray, down on his luck, to a cherished and pampered feline companion, Polar Bear takes his place among the most celebrated cats in recent literature. I was working at Cleveland's Fund for Animals on West Fifty-Seventh Street, where Polar Bear was a frequent office visitor. Cleveland and Polar Bear adored each other. Cleveland would tuck him in his jacket, bring him into the office, and stop by each desk to show Polar Bear what everyone was doing. We could all see they were a loving team.

When I would cat sit for Polar Bear, I had a chance to interact with him one-on-one, but only to a certain point. He was selective, but once he "approved" my presence he was courteous and polite. However, it was obvious to all of us that his true affections lay with Cleveland. Although his every need was provided for, Polar Bear remained very much his own cat.

Lessons from Polar Bear

We have all seen one-person cats; in fact, it is quite common. The best way to deal with that is to respect their relationship. Cats cannot and will not be forced into anything, and they tend not to do well in crowds. If you want a friend's cat to warm up to you, be sure to give him plenty of time and be patient.

MAKING A HAPPY HOME

Once you have decided that you are going to adopt a cat, you'll want to prepare a room that provides everything he needs—including a sense of safety and security. This will allow your cat to adjust to his new environment at his own pace. You will also want to cat-proof your home so that your feline friend is truly safe.

Preparing Your Home

Before you bring your new kitty home, prepare a room that includes a full litter box, water and food, treats, toys, and a scratching post to encourage good habits (and furniture protection). Feed him the diet he has been used to and then, as desired, gradually add any new food to the bowl. (See Chapter 2 for more about feeding kitty.) Always have plenty of clean, fresh water available. Once your new cat is placed in his room, don't force him out, and keep the door closed so that he feels safe in his little sanctuary.

While your cat is adjusting to his protected area, spend some time cat-proofing the rest of your home and start using kitty-safe behavior. Keep cleaning chemicals in a tightly closed cabinet or out of reach, and secure your cats in a separate room while cleaning. Remember, kitties lick their paws, so whatever they step into gets ingested. Be ready to keep your toilet seat and lid down from now on, because kittens can easily fall in. Your washers, dryers, and dishwashers should be checked before starting or closing them. Cats love to jump into enclosed spaces and especially like warm laundry. Check reclining chairs and dresser

When you bring a new cat home, always place him in a separate room that has been outfitted with a full litter box, water and food, treats, toys, and a scratching post. This will give him a sense of security while he begins adjusting to his new environment.

Roscoe and Bandit Share the Love

People often ask me if I think male cats are more affectionate than females. I have always had both and have found them equally loving. I once rescued two tiny kittens, a boy and a girl, from a busy construction site. Now grown up, Roscoe and Bandit are very spoiled (as they should be), and both like to sit on my lap at the same time. At fifteen pounds each, there is not much lap left. I believe if you give cats a lot of love, you will get it all back and more. That is certainly true in my home.

Feline Fact

Hard-working cats came to North America aboard the ships of European settlers, who used their feline companions as mouse catchers—first on ships, and later in homes, barns, and warehouses.

drawers before closing them, too. Make sure that paper shredders are unplugged and that all electrical wires are secured and out of the way. I suggest putting double-sided tape on items you don't want broken, or simply placing breakable treasures out of harm's way until your cat learns that they're off-limits. This will also protect kittens from being hurt by broken objects. Finally, place plants safely out of reach, especially if you have plants that are toxic to cats. (For more tips about houseplants, see pages 90 to 91 of Chapter 6.)

Introducing Your Cat to Your Home

Please understand that your new cat will need time to adjust. She may hide at first, which is normal, but she will come out to explore when ready. Don't force her out.

I think it is always best to introduce family members slowly. If you have young children, make sure they understand that the cat is not a doll, and they should not chase her or try to pull her tail. This is irresistible to some young children but is definitely not a favorite of any cat I know. Children can be shown the joy of loving, petting, and brushing cats, but also taught not to bother them while they are trying to eat, drink, rest, or use the litter box. A little common sense goes a long way.

I am a great believer in talking to my cats. A calm voice can be very reassuring. Cat food treats are another nice way to reward any good behavior and show your cat that you are a loving owner. Also play with

Feline Fact

Although kittens use meows to make their needs known, adult cats rarely meow at other cats. They reserve these vocalizations for humans, who respond best to verbal communication.

no Tarantulas Please

I once had a client who asked me if I would care for her boyfriend's cat, Max, while he was away. So far so good. She then added, "I should warn you, he also has a tarantula." Well, I had the same reaction anyone would, but being a game person, I decided to give it a try. The tarantula was kept in a huge glass tank with a very secure lid—I made certain of that before I agreed to come in and take care of the cat. Fortunately, I didn't have to take care of the tarantula! There were so many branches and icky things in his tank that I never saw him—which was fine with me—but I prayed Max did not know how to get the tank lid off. You never know.

It did not help my nerves that the apartment house itself was dark and creepy. In fact, it looked like the perfect setting for a horror movie. I grew to dread each house call, and every time I thought I saw something out of the corner of my eye, I jumped. Anyway, I got through it, but let me tell you, once is enough. I have had several clients with cats who share space with the more exotic variety of pets, but this was definitely the scariest I ever encountered.

and pet your new kitty as much as she will allow, but don't be too forceful. When she feels comfortable, you will have a friend for life. Lastly, exercise prudence with your new family member and enjoy this special time.

Creating an Emergency Plan

To prepare for a fire or other crisis, create an emergency plan that includes your feline friend. Put together a list of pet-friendly motels and disaster shelters, and fill a bag with all the essentials, including food, bottled water, collapsible bowls, and a disposable litter box and litter.

Now that your family has a new member (or two), it's smart to create an emergency plan that includes your feline companion. I once had to race up four flights of stairs in a smoke-filled building to rescue a cat named Queenie. A wonderful fireman helped me, and Queenie was saved. This story has a happy ending because even though Queenie's owner was not home, someone knew she was in the apartment.

I suggest that you put your emergency plan in writing and tape it to the refrigerator. This should include important phone numbers, pet-friendly motels, and disaster shelters that take cats. Then fill a bag with several days' worth of pet food and bottled water, plus collapsible pet bowls and a disposable litter box with litter. You can also get a front door label from the ASPCA that says animals are inside the home. Make sure you have a carrier for each pet, and keep the carriers accessible. Tape an up-to-date copy of your cat's vaccinations to the bottom.

A collar with an ID tag is critical in case you get separated from your pet. In addition, have your vet insert a microchip—a small device imprinted with a registered number that is placed under your cat's skin as a permanent means of identification. If your pet ends up at a shelter, the staff will scan for a microchip, so it provides added insurance in the unhappy event of a separation.

Above all, if an emergency occurs, try to stay calm. Cats can sense when something is wrong, and you will have a much easier time persuading your kitty to get into the carrier if she isn't spooked. A little catnip couldn't hurt.

CREATING A MULTI-PET HOUSEHOLD

Over the years, I have visited households that happily combined several cats, dogs and cats, birds and cats, and—in one case—a cat and a tarantula (which I do *not* recommend). The following guidelines will help you create a safe and harmonious home for your feline friend and other small animals (including cats) that your cat might instinctively be drawn to.

Introducing Your New Cat to Your Other Cats

Cats are territorial creatures and are never too thrilled when there is a change in their home scene, particularly when it involves sharing their cherished space with a brand new kitty. However, there are ways to make the introduction and assimilation easier on all parties, including you!

I suggest that when you arrange a separate room for your new cat, you prepare to keep the newcomer in it for at least a week. Cats react very strongly to smell, so get something that has your resident cat's scent on it, like a pet blanket, and put it in the newcomer's room. The reverse should be done as well so that each cat can grow accustomed to the other's scent. Do not change any of your resident cat's routines,

To pave the way for the introduction of your new cat to your resident pets, allow your pets to explore something that bears the newcomer's scent. One good way to do this is to allow resident pets to explore the carrier in which you brought the adoptee home.

such as feeding and grooming, and make sure you leave her litter box where it is. She has enough to deal with.

When you bring the new kitty home, put him in his room. Do not bring him to your resident cat for inspection—you are asking for trouble. With the door closed, let the two cats sniff under the door first; remember, smells are very important to a cat's psyche. When you decide to open the door for a short while, don't hover and try not to be nervous. Both cats will sense something is wrong. There is likely to be hissing and arched backs at first, so be patient. You can also try stacking two pet gates on top of each other when the doorway is open. That way, the cats can see and sniff safely but avoid a confrontation.

When your cats come face to face, have extra treats on hand—I am all for bribes. Eventually, you should be able to let both kitties interact without supervision. They might not be best buddies, but hopefully, feline harmony will allow them to coexist.

Pete Gets a New Playmate

One of my clients had two elderly cats, Wheatland and Pete. When Wheatland passed away, Pete seemed lonely and depressed. My client decided to adopt a seven-month-old cutey named Oskar to keep Pete company. With Oskar in the house, Pete soon became more like his old self. Just watching Oskar zoom around was like having a floor show staged especially for him.

Introducing Your New Cat to Your Dog

Interestingly enough, nearly half of all homes with pets have both cats and dogs, according to the American Veterinary Medical Association. Personally, I have found that introducing cats to dogs can be easier than cats to cats. Since I have always had both, it's a necessity that everyone gets along in my house.

With your new cat still in his "safe room," set up a pet gate in the doorway of the room and let your dog and cat see each other through the gate. (Be there to make sure neither jumps over it, please.) Don't force a get-together—see how they react with the gate separating them. After a number of days, put your dog on a leash, take down the gate, and let your cat come out for the meet and greet when he is ready.

Feline Fact
Unlike dogs, who alternate sides when they step, cats move both their left feet forward, followed by both their right feet. This gives them their characteristic smooth, elegant, often silent gait.

Ziggy and Ethel Play House

When I adopted my dog, Ziggy, felines were new to him and they looked like they would be fun to chase. After two days of firmly telling him "No," he understood that chasing wasn't allowed. Today, he has a loving relationship with all my cats, particularly Ethel, who thinks he is swell.

Make sure his nails are trimmed—although he will lash out only if he feels threatened—and steadily increase the time that the two are together without the gate. Hopefully, in time, they will cohabit peacefully. Also, please teach your dog that a cat is not for chasing. That will not lead to a lasting friendship.

If you already have cats and want to adopt a dog, I suggest choosing a small one with a calm, easy-going temperament. An older dog rather than a puppy would be best. Bring something with the new dog's scent home to your cats prior to his arrival, and vice versa, if you can. It's best to get them accustomed to each other's scents early on.

Feline Fact

Known as *nose leather*, the triangular tip at the end of a cat's nose may be pink or black. Like a human fingerprint, every cat's noseprint is unique.

Prepare a room with all the essentials for your cats—food, water, toys, litter—while your dog is getting acclimated. Also, prepare a separate room for the new dog and make sure it has a pet gate. Allow the dog to explore his new home while on a leash with supervision from you. After he is back in his room, let your cats out to smell where their new roommate has roamed; their noses will be on high speed. In time, hopefully, all will be able to coexist. Don't force them together, and always remain calm; anxiety can affect pets in a negative way. Know that a peaceful relationship requires time, patience, and love.

Introducing Your New Cat
to Birds, Fish, and Other Animals

If you have birds, hamsters, or fish, place the cage or tank where your cat can't tip it over. If you have a fish tank—and many people keep small animals in fish tanks—make sure it has a very secure top. Provide items in the tank or cage that can act as hiding places so that your small pets can relax.

You need patience, and you must be on your guard because every pet has to feel safe in his home. Also, know that trouble can work both ways. Yes, cats are predators, but large parrots, for example, have powerful beaks and can cause real damage if your cat sticks her paws in the cage. Make sure the cage bars are close enough together to prevent a paw from squeezing in. Lastly, keep your small animals and birds behind closed doors and away from your kitty when you go out. There is no need to tempt the innate curiosity of our feline friends. With preparation and care, you should enjoy a harmonious household.

Adopting a cat has always been a "win-win" in my household. I have given many cats a good home, and I cannot even begin to tell you how much they have given back in sincere and unconditional love and friendship. I wish you the same with your new kitties.

Feeding Kitty

From finicky cats to those who eat like panthers, our kitties have very definite ideas about food. As a cat sitter, I have seen every variety of feline food preferences, and owners who try to accommodate them.

I remember when one of my clients decided to travel out of town for the Jewish holiday of Passover. It is one thing to keep kosher for the holidays, but expecting your cats to do the same can be tricky for a cat sitter. My client left detailed instructions that her two pampered Persians, Jasmine and Theodore, were to observe the Jewish holiday dietary rules as well. This was a first, but I always try to follow my client's wishes. She left out matzo and sardines with instructions to serve them on paper plates using plastic utensils.

Although Jasmine and Theodore were used to being treated as family members, not just felines, they would not touch the matzo, and I was afraid to give them sardines because that can sometimes cause diarrhea. I ended up going to a supermarket with a kosher deli section and buying some nice cold cuts, which I then wrapped around the matzo. They were very fond of the deli cuts but only picked at the unleavened cracker in the center. As soon as the holiday was over, they went back to their regular food, though I understand they frequently lobbied for more kosher deli.

In my many years as a cat sitter, I have been asked to cater to all sorts of cats, and I have been asked all sorts of food questions regarding all sorts of kitties. In this chapter, I am happy to share some tips on keeping your cat's cuisine healthy and appetizing.

THE BASICS

Always choose high-quality cat foods that list protein, such as chicken or fish, as the primary ingredient. Proteins are your cat's main source of energy and the building blocks of muscles and other tissues.

I often say that cats do not ask too much from us, but making sure they get the right food and nutrition is essential. There are all kinds of food choices available today. Some people prefer to give their cats canned food, others prefer dry, and some choose a mixture of both. Unless your cat has special dietary concerns, I believe it is really an individual choice—yours and your kitty's. There are some dietary basics, though, that you should keep in mind.

- Buy high-quality cat foods that have protein (chicken, fish, or another meat) as the first ingredient. Although it may be tempting to feed human food to your feline companion, for the most part, your kitty's diet should be made up of commercial cat food, which contains taurine and other essential amino acids and nutrients that cats need to stay healthy.

🐾 Choose food that is appropriate for your cat's age. Kittens need a food that is especially rich in protein, calcium, and other nutrients. As cats get older, their nutritional needs change and require extra consideration. If you're not sure what your cat should be eating, speak to your veterinarian.

🐾 Feed your cat in dishes made of stainless steel or lead-free ceramic or pottery—not plastic, because bacteria can develop in the scratches, causing acne and chin rash. I suggest washing the food and water bowls every day.

🐾 Don't leave wet food out all day. Just put down enough for your cat to finish in one sitting.

🐾 Be sure to refrigerate any leftover canned cat food. I suggest transferring the leftovers to a small airtight plastic container before storing in the refrigerator. These foods just keep better in plastic than in the can.

🐾 Provide plenty of fresh water to keep your cat hydrated. I always have clean water available throughout the house for my kitties. (For more about water, see page 29.)

🐾 If the cost of cat food is an issue, buy in bulk, check the Sunday papers and online sites for sales, inquire about special deals at your

Water is an essential part of a cat's diet, especially if she eats mostly dry food. Provide plenty of fresh water for your cat, and, if necessary, encourage her to drink by putting ice cubes in her dish or purchasing a kitty water fountain.

local supermarket and pet store, and ask friends who do not have cats to clip coupons. You would be surprised at how much you can save this way. I once saved thirty dollars—all from extra coupons I received from friends.

Farrah and Delilah Favor Waterford

I once had a client who insisted I serve food to her kitties, Farrah and Delilah, in Waterford crystal goblets. No joke. The cats didn't know the difference, of course, but I sure did. I was terrified to wash the goblets for fear I would drop one. I managed to keep them intact, but cleaning up was always a bit stressful.

Common Dietary Concerns and Habits

Feline Fact
A cat is unable to see an object that's directly under her nose. That's why cats sometimes can't seem to find tidbits that have been placed on the floor in front of them.

Every cat is unique, with her own quirks and preferences. Just the same, I've noticed that many of my clients raise the same concerns and issues about their cat's diet and eating habits.

Some cats are very aggressive about stealing people food, sometimes right in front of us. I suggest you do not allow your kitty on top of any table where you serve food—that will only encourage him to misbehave. As already mentioned, your cat should eat commercial cat food only, except under special circumstances. When cats get picky or have special needs due to illness or age, certain people food is fine as long as your veterinarian approves. To avoid temptation, put leftovers away promptly. Try to wash the dishes as soon as possible or you might find your cat licking the dirty plates—you know how they always try to be helpful!

People seem to associate milk with a cat's diet. I think a little fat-free milk will not hurt some cats, and a teaspoon of plain yogurt every now and then as a treat is fine. However, many cats are lactose intolerant and if they drink cow's milk, they will end up with an upset stomach or diarrhea. The fact is that adult cats do not need milk in their diets. Kittens require their mother's milk to grow strong and healthy. If you've rescued pre-weaned kittens, they need feline milk replacement formula, which is sold in pet stores or the pet food section of supermarkets. If your cat has already been weaned, though, it's better to give her a healthy treat that's made just for felines.

The best beverage for your cat is clean water. If you don't think she is drinking enough of it, try adding some to her wet food to make a yummy gravy. I am also very fond of water fountains made for cats, found in most pet stores. I have several in my house and my cats love them. Cats appear to be attracted to the sound and movement of running water—many love to lick drops from a faucet or sit at the edge of a tub and swat the water stream—so fountains can entice them into drinking more. One kitty I care for named Sugar enjoys splashing the water out of her water bowls. She does this so much that her owners now keep her bowls in the bathtub! While you might not want your cat to be quite that playful with her water bowl, a fun trick is to put ice cubes in the dish. This creates an entertaining game and will encourage her to drink more.

Although you may love the image of a cat lapping up milk or cream from a saucer, adult cats don't need milk, and many are unable to digest cow's milk.

Feline Fact

Unlike a dog, who uses the tongue as a scoop when lapping up water, a cat uses just the tip of the tongue to pull water upwards to his mouth. He then snaps his jaw shut before gravity can pull the liquid back to earth. This requires a good bit of coordination.

While we're talking about our feline friends' fascination with water, I can't emphasize enough how important it is to keep the toilet seat lid down, especially if you have curious kittens. You do not want your kitty drinking toilet water, which might contain toxic cleaning chemicals or harmful bacteria.

Maddie's Eating Disorder

Maddie didn't just lap up her food, she would eat anything—string, bottle caps, ribbon, plants—anything she could get her paws on. But her true passion was plastic bags. She once ingested an entire kitchen garbage bag which, fortunately, was just too much for her stomach and came out in a twisted mass. It is a miracle Maddie did not succumb to her bizarre cravings, but her poor owners were always on high alert!

FUSSY EATERS

There is little that frustrates a cat owner more than a fussy eater. I've seen owners pray that their kitty would reward them by eating something—anything! The good news is that patience and the willingness to try different brands and flavors can pay off.

This was certainly true of a cat named Sophie, who was fifteen years old with a thyroid condition and was on medication. I once cared for her twice a day for over a month, and because she was thin and a fussy eater, her owners left me a mountain of canned food to try. I had no idea which would appeal to her finicky appetite (and I am not sure she did either).

As I offered each can of food, I kept a daily diary of what she liked or didn't, and how much she ate. This worked for both of us, as I determined what her favorites were. I also noted in the diary how alert she was and what her daily litter box habits were. You can imagine how many pages this produced.

Sophie's owners were so delighted with her well-documented desires that they continued her daily diary. If your cat is hale and hearty, a diary is not all that necessary, but for an ailing cat, it can be very important—especially for your vet.

The best way to introduce a food to your kitties is to mix the new food in with the old, and then gradually reduce the portion of the old food. This can be done over a period of several days or a week, and gives your cat a chance to adjust to the new menu. Hopefully, he will give it "two paws up."

If your cat does not eat the way she used to due to age or illness, there are several tricks that may entice her back to the food bowl. Please note, however, that if your cat has stopped eating for forty-eight hours, you should call your vet right away.

If your cat is a fussy eater, try warming her food slightly. Making the food more "smelly" may stimulate kitty's appetite.

🐾 Warm your cat's canned food slightly. Cats seem to like warm food, which gives off a more appealing smell than cold or room-temperature fare. Since smell stimulates the appetite, this could get your fussy kitty's attention. You can also mix some hot water or chicken broth into the food, which will both warm it up and make a scrumptious gravy.

☙ Choose a really smelly canned food, such as one that includes tuna or mackerel. This is especially helpful for cats who are suffering from colds for the simple reason that they will be able to smell the food much more easily.

☙ Put a small amount of food on your cat's chin or mouth to see if he will lick it off.

☙ Try adding cooked chicken livers to your cat's food. Liver has a very strong smell.

Feline Fact

In addition to smelling with their nose, cats can smell with a special structure called the *Jacobson's organ.* Because this feature is located on the upper surface of the mouth, cats must slightly open their mouth to use it.

☙ Place a few cat food treats on top of your cat's regular food.

☙ Try a small dish of baby food, which is irresistible to many cats. Do not choose vegetable flavors—chicken or meat is fine. Baby food is great to stimulate the appetite but should not be used as a main food source.

☙ To awaken your cat's appetite and enhance nutrition, offer one of the high-calorie pastes sold in pet stores and online. Mix it with cat food or put it on your fingers so that your cat can lick it off. Most kitties seem to like the taste.

WHEN WEIGHT PROBLEMS ADD UP TO TROUBLE

Cats come in all shapes and sizes, but it is best to keep them to a reasonable weight. Like humans, cats find it very easy to put on the pounds, but it is very difficult for owners to get those pounds off.

Sometimes, our kitties can give us an unexpected and amusing wake-up call. I remember cat sitting for Simon, a large orange tabby in a multi-cat household. He had his own litter box with a hood, but whenever I arrived to care for him, I would find the hood off the box and dumped in another area of the home. I could not figure out how it got there.

Well, the mystery was solved one day when I followed him to the litter box. Poor Simon had become so fat, he could squeeze through the hood opening but could not get out again without getting stuck. So he would leap out, hood and all, and waddle through the house until the hood finally dislodged itself somewhere. Needless to say, Simon was put on a diet and received a new litter box without a hood!

There are some cats who just can't eat enough and some owners who just can't say no. An overweight cat is going to have health problems, so please try to keep the weight down. Your vet can tell you the ideal weight for your cat and can also recommend a good diet. Just like us, however, cats don't love dietary restrictions. Be patient, because it has been my experience that weight loss is usually gradual—in fact, it *must* be gradual because sudden weight loss can cause serious illness and can even be fatal to a cat. Please know that your efforts will be rewarded because you will be sparing your plump kitty's joints as she gets older. Excess weight can also lead to diabetes.

Buddy Packs on the Pounds

Buddy was a gray tabby. He had a pretty outdoor garden to play in, so his owner kept him in a cat harness full-time. However, she neglected to adjust it as he started to gain weight. One day, I picked him up and the harness was so tight, I was surprised he could move. We couldn't even unbuckle it and had to finally cut it off. As Buddy leapt to freedom, he dashed around the house several times in pure celebration. He has since gotten a plus-size harness.

If your vet has told you that kitty needs to lose a few pounds, the following tips should prove helpful:

If your kitty is overweight, look for weight-control cat foods, which are available in both wet and dry varieties at your supermarket and pet supply store. If your cat is significantly overweight, ask your veterinarian to recommend a "prescription" weight-loss formula.

- If your cat is slightly overweight or you want to maintain a healthy weight, look for a weight-control cat food. These are available in both wet and dry varieties and can be purchased in pet stores and sometimes even in supermarkets. Make sure that your vet approves of the choice.

- If your cat is significantly overweight, choose a weight-loss formula that can be purchased only through a veterinarian. Your vet can tell you which formula is appropriate for your kitty.

- Make time for play every day. Interactive play is a great way to bond with your kitty and can take off unwanted pounds—sometimes yours along with his. For ideas on inexpensive, fun cat toys and activities, as well as important safety tips, turn to Chapter 7, "Playtime and Special Occasions."

- Don't abandon the use of edible treats. All my clients know that I am a big believer in cat treats, which provide a wonderful way to reward your kitties for good behavior, pamper them, and provide a little extra TLC. However, for an overweight cat, I suggest that you stick to diet treats (yes, they sell them) and limit the amount you offer each day.

- Feed only a few small meals a day and remove the food in between feedings. If you are not home to do this, try an automatic feeder, which will dispense a measured amount of food at programmed intervals.

- Finely chop some lettuce and add it to your cat's food. He will feel like he is getting more to eat. A vet provided this tip years ago, and it works like magic with some cats.

- Switch to wet cat food, which has fewer calories and is higher in protein than dry food. Another option is to simply provide less dry and more canned fare.

To bulk up your overweight kitty's wet food, try mixing in some finely chopped lettuce. He'll feel like he's getting more food.

Wilbur Builds a Moat

On my first house call to care for Wilbur, a tabby, I was shocked to see ants crawling around his food bowl. I had to do something. Remembering my history classes, I put all the food dishes on a cookie sheet and then filled the perimeter with water, basically creating a moat. It worked! Other clients have adopted the moat defense when needed.

DISTINCTIVE FELINE
FARFEL VS. THE TURKEY

 I remember one Thanksgiving, when it was my turn to cook dinner for a large crowd. I had a twenty-pound turkey in the sink, all ready to be dressed and put into a nice hot oven. I left the kitchen for just a minute to check on something in another room, but when I returned, there was my cat Farfel with his back legs perched on the kitchen counter and front legs in the sink! What a sight. Worse, his teeth were sunk into my bird, and even though it weighed twice as much as he did, he was trying to drag it out of the sink.

When I saw Farfel, I asked, "What do you think you are doing?" He looked up at me as if to say, "Wait, I saw it first!" Anyway, he quickly scampered off without causing too much damage to the turkey, and I was able to carefully cut off the small piece that bore his tiny but distinct tooth marks. I gave him some extra cat treats as a reward for letting me reclaim my turkey. Thanksgiving was saved, and Farfel did enjoy some special turkey-flavored treats after all the festivities were over.

Lessons from Farfel

Whenever a cat sets his mind on something you don't approve of, be prepared to stand firm, especially if it involves food. I am now careful to keep a sharp eye on both my feline friends and my kitchen during any food preparations, and especially on festive occasions. Having extra cat treats on hand helps prevent temptation.

The tips presented earlier in this chapter will help reduce or control weight in most circumstances, but if you live in a multi-cat household, you will face an additional challenge: How can you keep your overweight kitty on a diet without compromising the health of his feline housemate? If all kitties behaved themselves at dinnertime and ate just what was in their own bowls without eyeing what everyone else was munching on, it would be easy to keep one cat on a diet while allowing the other one to eat at will. Since this is not usually the case, I always suggest feeding cats separately and putting your slimmer cat's food in a place that's too small for your corpulent kitty to enter. Overweight cats have trouble jumping onto surfaces, so you can also try placing your thinner cat's food up on a counter. That being said, double-check with your vet to make sure that kitty's inability to jump doesn't have a cause other than excess weight.

Remember that your cat's weight loss must be gradual because sudden weight loss can cause serious illness. Never put your kitty on a crash diet.

As long as you use a little common sense and keep an eye on proper nutrition, your cats can enjoy a diet that is tasty, healthy, and beneficial. They say food is love, and one look at dinnertime in my household of contented kitties certainly confirms it.

Indoor/Outdoor Adventures

I believe that cats have a better life indoors, away from fleas and ticks, diseases, pesticides, garbage, dogs, speeding cars, and a variety of other hazards. Indoor cats live fifteen years or longer on average. If you're like me, you want to keep your kitties with you for as long as possible.

I had one client who allowed her cat, Merlin, to go into her private outdoor garden through an open window that was protected by safety bars. Merlin could *just* squeeze through. Luckily, the garden was completely enclosed; otherwise, leaving a window open in Manhattan is a total no-no. Still, it bothered me, and I asked if she would keep Merlin inside while she was away. I was worried that when I did my house

As a rule, cats should be kept indoors, where they are safe from other cats and dogs, fleas, diseases, cars, and many other hazards.

calls, the kitty would be outside and I would never see him. Unfortunately, she said that since Merlin was used to being outside, she didn't want to keep him in, adding that he would be "just fine." Famous last words . . .

On my second visit, I discovered, to my horror, that Merlin was quite the hunter. I walked in to find pigeon feathers everywhere and what was left of the poor, dead bird on the floor. It was an awful sight. I cleaned it up, grimacing all the way. I guess Merlin was bringing me a gift—but it was one I could have lived without!

As a cat owner, one of the most important decisions you will make is whether to let your cat outdoors. As I said, I feel that indoors is best, but with a few adjustments to your home, your kitty might just have the best of both worlds.

GIVING YOUR CAT THE BEST OF BOTH WORLDS

I am often asked if it is okay to take an indoor cat outside to a local park or into a garden. As a rule, I do not recommend it. I know it is tempting to imagine your kitty soaking up the sun and frolicking in the grass, but what seems pleasant to you can be potentially dangerous for your pet. Outdoor parks and even private backyards very often have fleas, ticks, and other parasites just waiting to hitch a ride on your cat. Sometimes, there can be pet dogs off their leashes, and in more rustic areas, parks are home to raccoons, coyotes, and other wild creatures. Also, the outside world can be noisy, and cats are easily frightened, particularly of unfamiliar sights and sounds. Sometimes when I am out walking through Central Park in New York City, I see people with cat carriers trying to coax their kitties out. More often than not, the cats are having a miserable time. I even saw someone put a cat in a pet stroller with nylon mesh. It was unusual, but certainly creative.

There is a reason why cats love "home sweet home." Their own familiar space, filled with small, cozy hideaways like boxes, bags, or cat beds, makes them feel safe and secure. Because they love vertical spaces, you can further enhance their home environment by adding cat trees and perches, which will help your feline friend enjoy the smallest of living areas. If you want to introduce a bit of nature, try getting a small bird feeder with a suction cup that can be attached to the outside of his favorite window. Kitty will love watching the birds while safely channeling his inner tiger. To make that windowsill even more attractive, turn it into a perch. Pet stores sell special window seats, but you could easily make one yourself by getting a board wide enough to comfortably fit a kitty, wrap-

Feline Fact

Cats like high places
because they provide a
better observation
point and a sense of
security. In a multi-cat
household, the cat on
the highest perch is
usually the "top cat."

ping the top and sides in carpet or another soft material, and attaching it securely to your windowsill. Talk about cozy! You might also plant some indoor kitty grass for him—my cats love it. Also please make sure all window screens are in good repair and firmly secured. As I often say, cats do not come equipped with parachutes!

Hermes and Snookie Like City Life

Hermes and Snookie live in a tiny studio apartment with a huge window facing a busy street. Their owner has given each a multi-level carpeted tree house right by the window where they can perch up high and watch the world go by. Cats do just fine in small spaces as long as you make them interesting.

Years ago, when I lived in a house with a yard and reverse commuted into Manhattan to do my house calls (that's another story), I actually had an outdoor cat enclosure attached to the side of my house. Accessible from the house and completely enclosed with wire, it had perches inside for my cats to sit on, and part of a tree for them to scratch on while they enjoyed the outdoors in safety. A little research on the Internet or in pet stores will show you what's available. Just make sure there is no way for your cats to escape!

If you really want to try to bring your indoor kitty outside, your own backyard is best. The following guidelines should help keep her safe and sound.

- Please make sure that your cat has all her shots, and check with your vet to see if she needs more vaccinations to go outdoors.

- Take kitty out under supervision, wearing a harness with a leash. Make sure it's a small cat harness, not one intended for a small dog. Before your first outdoor adventure, get her used to the harness by having her wear it inside for short intervals each day.

- In case of escape, fit your cat with a collar that includes an ID tag and—in consideration of our feathered friends—a small bell.

- Check the ASPCA website (www.aspca.org/pet-care/poison-control/plants/) for a current list of plants that are toxic to cats, and steer your cat away from any harmful flora. Remember that even plants not on the list may have been sprayed with pesticides that can hurt your kitty.

- Keep your eye out for fleas, which are more likely to be a problem when pets go outdoors. (See the inset on page 44 for information on flea control.)

The safest way to allow your cat to enjoy the outdoors is an outdoor cat enclosure. Just make sure that kitty can't escape and that no other animals can enter!

TRAVEL AND YOUR CAT

Cats do not like being in confined spaces, and since many of us bring out a cat carrier only when we take them to the vet, it becomes double trouble in their eyes. My orange kitty Sammy is a feisty, big boy with strong opinions, including opinions about the carrier, as in "no way." I've always found that carriers with an opening on the top are easier than ones with front openings, particularly when dealing with reluc-

CONTROLLING FLEAS

Years ago when I was very involved with animal rescue, I had a real flea infestation in my house, and it was not pleasant. Fleas are hardy buggers and can attach themselves to clothing and shoes. Little did I know that when I was outside helping animals, I was also bringing some unwelcome "guests" back inside. If your kitty goes outside—or if you or anyone who visits your home has pets who spend time out-of-doors—you, too, may eventually have to deal with fleas, both on your cat and in your home.

There are many good products that can help rid your kitty of fleas. Available from your local vet and from pet stores, they include topical treatments, which are placed between the shoulder blades, as well as oral tablets and flea sprays. And there is always flea shampoo, but I don't recommend that for the faint of heart. Baths and cats are usually not a happy mix, so I do suggest a professional groomer or at least a helpful friend if you decide to take the shampoo route.

Meanwhile, I have a suggestion that does not require sprays and soaps, and has worked for me throughout the years—brewer's yeast. I learned about it from a friend who has a large farm in Pennsylvania. She cares for a colony of feral cats, all of whom are spayed and neutered. We all want to help control the cat population. Even though my friend has names for all her furry charges, she can't get close enough to administer flea treatments. Fortunately, she discovered that sprinkling brewer's yeast with garlic on their dry food helped with flea control. It seems that the odor of the yeast as it is being digested repels the fleas! Both powder and tablet forms are available in health food and pet supply stores. Sprinkle the powder over your cat's regular food, or use the tablets as treats. The brewer's yeast will help keep kitty's coat healthier, so you will get a double benefit.

As always, check with your vet as to which flea-control products are safe. Never use a dog product on a cat, and always follow weight and age requirements to the letter. If your kitty wears a flea collar, make sure it is not too close to the skin because it can cause irritations. Also remember to remove the excess portion of the collar after determining the right size for your cat. Be especially careful when treating home infestations, which may require special sprays and flea bombs. Fleas can cause nasty diseases, but the misuse of insecticides can be just as dangerous for your feline friend.

tant cats. But when it came time to take Sammy to the vet one day, I remembered I had loaned my top-opener to a friend, and it hadn't yet been returned. My only choice was a front-opening carrier.

Well, the ensuing battle wasn't pretty. I finally got Sammy in rear-end first, and it wasn't until I was at the vet's office that we noticed blood on the carrier. It was mine. Sammy had landed a deep scratch before his undignified transport. I finally cured Sammy of his frantic response by making the carrier another part of his normal environment. I found a quiet place in one of my rooms where I could leave it open and let him explore. After I added some bedding and a favorite catnip toy, he started to view it as another place to enjoy a snooze. We no longer have carrier wars.

This story has a happy ending, but unfortunately, that is not always the case. However, I do have some suggestions that may help you win the carrier wars—or at least negotiate a truce—and guide you in making travel easier, whether it is to the vet, to a vacation home, or to a new home.

Choosing a Cat Carrier

There are all kinds of considerations when purchasing a carrier. Carriers come in all sizes and shapes, but I have found that cats are more likely to go into one that is large enough to allow them to stand up and turn around. This is especially important if you intend to take your cat on long car trips. Some carriers have a door on the top, some have one in the front, and some have both. As already mentioned, I prefer top openings, which make it easier to put your cat in and take him out. This

Feline Fact

It has been scientifically proven that you can lower both your blood pressure and your heart rate by stroking a purring cat. Unfortunately, research has failed to explain *how* cats make that wonderful purring sound.

If you have trouble getting kitty in and out of the carrier, choose a model with an opening on top instead of the side. Many carriers have both top and side openings.

is especially helpful at the vet's, where getting a resistant kitty out—or worse, dumping him on the exam table—can be very stressful.

Whatever type of carrier you choose, make sure it has good ventilation and a secure door and latch. You don't want your cat getting out unexpectedly. Cat carriers with wheels on the bottom are easier when you're dealing with a very large cat, but tend to tilt the kitty during transport and can make a lot of noise as the wheels move.

As already said, getting a cat into a carrier can be quite an adventure, especially if the carrier appears only occasionally to take him somewhere he doesn't want to go. Try getting your kitty used to his carrier by leaving it out in a quiet, tucked-away place. Put a favorite blanket, pillow, or other bedding inside, along with catnip and a few toys and treats. This will make the carrier appear more like a fun hangout. In fact, one of my carriers is so inviting that my cat Bandit enjoyed sleeping in it. There she was, snoozing away, when I had to take her brother, Roscoe, to the vet. I had to lure Bandit out with a trail of treats. Roscoe then went in willingly, and, of course, he got a treat as well. If

To eliminate or reduce carrier fears, furnish your carrier with bedding, a catnip toy, and treats, and leave it open in a quiet area of your home. Then allow kitty to explore and take a cat nap in his new digs.

Dennis Prefers Stay-Cations

Very often, cats and cat carriers do not mix well, and that is particularly true of Dennis, a kitty I have been cat sitting for years. Although I try not to play favorites, I cannot help but love him. However, he does not travel well. His owners once tried to include him in a weekend trip to Cape Cod—a five-hour drive from New York City. After a solid hour of wailing, Dennis got his way and was returned home, never to journey north again.

you can't leave the carrier out all the time, try a few days a week, but make sure it contains all the fun things I mentioned. Also make sure to clean it out occasionally, particularly if it has bedding.

Taking Your Cat on Trips

One of my clients has four cats and has made very cute condos out of her cat carriers. When I arrive to take care of her kitties, I go over to a large window where she has the carriers stacked two by two, with bedding and toys on the inside, and a great view of Manhattan outside. Needless to say, when she travels to her country home with her cats, they are happy to go along.

Before attempting to take your cat on a long car trip for the holidays or a vacation, try a test drive. I have taken my carrier-shy kitties on short car trips to show them that the end result of a ride in the carrier can be good. Once you are ready to travel with your cat, make sure that the carrier contains everything she needs, including bedding, toys, and treats. Always keep her in the carrier when you are driving, and secure it with a seat belt threaded through the handle. If the carrier is large enough, you may be able to put a small litter pan inside. If not, take along a disposable litter box, sold in pet stores. When you stop the car, put litter or shredded newspaper in the box and, hopefully, your kitty will make use of it. These boxes also work well in a motel setting. Bring a supply of plastic garbage bags for easy disposal of waste.

To help prevent your cat from getting car sick, I suggest you remove all food and water by midnight before the journey, and ask your vet if motion sickness medicine is right for her. Always have drinking

Before taking your cat on a road trip, try a short test drive to show your feline friend that a car ride doesn't always mean a trip to the vet.

Toni Takes the Wheel

When you travel anywhere by car with your cat, please always put her in a cat carrier. A friend's niece adopted a kitten named Toni and thought she could just drive a few blocks with her new kitty unsecured. Toni had other ideas. As soon as the engine started, she panicked and got under the foot pedals. A small accident occurred, but fortunately, no one was hurt. After that, Toni traveled only in a carrier.

water available in plastic bottles that you can pour into a bowl during rest breaks, and never leave your cat unattended.

Leaving Your Cat at Home When You Travel

If at all possible, leave your cat at home while you travel, and arrange for a trusted friend or professional cat sitter to provide food, water, and clean litter.

Cats are most comfortable in their own environment, so if you have the option to leave your kitty at home when you travel, do so. It's much better than boarding. However, you need a professional cat sitter or a trusted friend to care for your kitty while you're away. The best way to find a cat sitter is through referrals. If you don't know anyone who uses a sitter, call your vet or local shelters. They should be able to supply a name or two. Make sure that the sitter comes to your house prior to the trip to meet your cat and see your feeding and litter routines, and always check references.

Cats are creatures of habit and love things to stay just the way they are. That said, when you leave for any length of time, they will miss you and the home routine you share. When I do my cat sitting, it's obvious that some cats are lonely, so I always like to give them a little extra TLC.

There are ways you can make it easier for your kitty when you travel. Leave a recently worn article of clothing near his favorite spot. Your scent will comfort him while you are away. I do not recommend leaving the TV on. The way many of these systems are designed now, anything could happen, including a power surge. Instead, I suggest leaving on a small radio, set on your favorite station.

One of my regular cat-sitting charges is an adorable tuxedo cat named Nicky. His owners have taken my advice and leave their radio on an all-news station when away. Not only does it comfort him, I often joke that Nicky is the best informed cat in New York City.

One neat thing some people do is call and leave messages for their kitties on their answering machine. I was visiting a home once when a call came in from an owner. The cat and I looked at the phone, and then each other, and I was sure I saw a contented kitty.

To keep your home-alone kitty from feeling lonely, leave a recently worn article of clothing near his favorite spot and tune a small radio to your (or his) favorite station. You can even call home to leave messages for him on your answering machine.

Making Your Cat Comfortable When Moving to a New Home

Moving can be very stressful for all of us, and with cats involved, it can be even more worrisome. There are some steps you can take to ease the pain, though.

On moving day, have a designated room in your old home for your cat, complete with his litter, food and water, toys, and something with your scent to lie on. Secure the door and put a sign on it that says "Do Not Open—Cat Inside!" You do not want the movers disturbing him during the process, and you don't want to take a chance on a panicky kitty escaping.

DISTINCTIVE FELINE
MOLLY—A BRAVE KITTY GETS HELP

Molly wasn't the kind of kitty you could go over and pet. If I got too close, she looked as if she was wondering what I was going to do to her. When cats are shy, I don't disturb them, because I'd rather have them feel secure and remain where I can keep an eye on them. "I'm not going to bother you, Molly, I just want to make sure you're okay," I would say to her. But on one visit, Molly seemed different—more than shy, she was lethargic and was obviously favoring a paw. I knew I had to find out what was wrong.

Molly was in pain, poor little kitty. I looked closely and found, to my horror, that one of her long, untrimmed nails was curling around full circle and growing through her paw pad. I brought her to the vet immediately. She had to anesthetize Molly and remove the nail surgically.

The kitty's owner was shocked when I told her what had happened. She did love Molly and always kept a stock of delicacies for her. She told me Molly wouldn't let her get near her claws, and she really didn't know it was that bad. Maybe she was overcompensating with the fancy food. The good news is that Molly got well and stopped being afraid of me. Maybe in a way, she realized I had helped her.

Lessons from Molly

Cats are stoic creatures who cannot tell us what is wrong. Although most owners mean well and would not intentionally hurt their kitties, occasionally, I do need to step in. I tell all my clients to check their kitty's nails and clip them if they get too long and pay attention if their behavior changes. Molly was a brave girl who suffered in silence, but I am glad that her story had a happy ending.

When it is time to move, place your cat in the carrier while he is still in the room. Put a toy in with him. Once you are in your new home, move your kitty into a pre-selected room that is as far as possible from the confusion. Make sure the room has already been set up with litter, food, toys, and something soft and familiar to lie on. Keep him there until everything has quieted down. Give him extra treats and some new toys (and a new scratching post) to make him feel special. Above all, be patient. Before letting your cat loose in a new home, make sure you have checked it thoroughly to ensure that it is safe and free from unwelcome escape routes. Let him leave the room and explore his new home when ready.

Like many of us, cats are homebodies. They are happiest in their own homes surrounded by familiar scents, sights, sounds, and toys. Keep in mind that you are part of their home, so if they have to travel or move, your presence is key to their adjustment. Provide them with love and consistency, and you will find them surprisingly adaptable.

When moving to a new home, keep kitty away from the noise and confusion by placing her in a pre-selected room that has been furnished with a litter box, food, water, toys, and treats. Most important, provide lots of TLC while she adjusts to her new surroundings.

Love Your Litter Box

Cats are extremely clean animals, and their fastidious nature almost always extends to their bathroom habits. However, people are always asking me about litter box problems, especially when their kitties suddenly stop using their boxes. This creates a very difficult home situation, and unfortunately, I have heard it is the number one reason why cats are given up by their owners.

It is true that cats can be picky in their bathroom habits, but I once had a client who was even pickier than her cat. Sandy was a very sweet orange tabby, and her owner had some very unusual instructions with regard to Sandy's litter box. First of all, she kept the litter box in the bathtub, and because she didn't want particles scattered around, she filled it with facial tissues instead of litter.

When I came to care for Sandy, I had to clean out her box and then carefully stack new tissues all over the inside, creating a fluffy, cloud-like effect. When it was time to clean the box, the tissues were soggy with urine and the white, fluffy cloud had turned into a yellow mess. I had to dump it all into a trash bag and wash out the box with bleach before replacing the tissue. I have to admit, though, that there was never a problem with odor in her apartment, and I never had to sweep up scattered litter. This was a very unusual solution and expensive to boot, but Sandy loved it, and why not? Her dainty tush was always comfortably cushioned by clouds!

This chapter presents practical advice I can offer as both a cat sitter and an owner. I hope that it will help you and your kitty stay on the same page as far as the litter box is concerned.

CHOOSING THE BEST LITTER BOX FOR YOUR CAT

When choosing a litter box, make sure it is roomy enough to allow your cat to turn around. Then place it in a quiet yet easy-to-access spot.

Litter boxes come in all sizes and shapes, covered and uncovered. My cats happen to love an uncovered oval box, a relatively new design. It's high on the sides and lower in the front, and I find the litter does not scatter as much. Also, with no corners, it's much easier to scoop. Whatever shape you decide to buy, please make sure the box is roomy enough to allow your cat to turn around. If you have multiple cats, have multiple boxes. I have even known cats that like two boxes of their own—one for number one and the other for number two. Place the boxes in quiet, easily accessible spots, but away from feeding bowls. Cats prefer a separate area for dining, which makes perfect sense.

Sasha Stands Guard

Sasha and Pippin were roommates but not pals. Sasha liked to pick on Pippin and would block the entrance to their hooded litter box when Pippin was using it. Trapped, Pippin would have to hustle to exit the box and get past Sasha. I was surprised that Pippin still used her commode, so I suggested that their owners get an uncovered litter box. Pippin was much happier.

If you are using a box with a hood, make sure it is tall enough for your cat to stand up in. Although I like hooded boxes—not as much litter gets sprayed over the floor—they have less ventilation and really do need daily attention. However, in a multi-cat household where the cats do not get along, one cat using a hooded box can get trapped by another cat standing at the opening. I have seen this happen. In that case, I recommend two boxes, one sans hood.

If you have a kitten, you cannot expect him to climb into a huge litter box designed for an adult cat. Check out the shallow boxes created especially for kittens and geriatric cats, both of whom may find it difficult to get in and out of a box with high sides. For healthy full-grown kitties, a high-sided litter box is great for preventing scattered litter.

Hooded litter boxes are great for preventing scatter. Just ensure that the hood is high enough for your cat to stand up.

CHOOSING THE BEST LITTER FOR YOUR CAT

Which litter is best, clumping or non-clumping? That really is an individual choice—yours and your cat's. I like the clumping litter, which

Feline Fact
Clay litter was invented by accident in the 1940s. When cat owner Kay Draper decided to try sawdust as a litter, Edward Lowe, a local sawmill worker, suggested the use of absorbent clay instead. Soon, cat owners were clamoring for this convenient product.

Unless your cat has a health disorder that requires a specific type of litter, use the product that your cat prefers. If he objects to the product's smell or feel, he may choose to do his business elsewhere.

forms a solid, easy-to-remove mass each time the cat urinates. It requires less maintenance and can be more economical in the long run. It lasts longer than a non-clumping product because you can scoop out the urine while the rest of the litter remains clean. It's also a good choice if your cat has urinary problems and you need to keep track of how often and how much he is peeing. If you find yourself scooping more clumps or larger clumps, you'll know that he is peeing more. Follow the directions as to the amount to put in each box. Even though this litter tends to control odor better than a non-clumping product, it should be scooped on a daily basis and changed completely every seven to ten days, please.

If you prefer non-clumping litter, be aware that the urine will soak through and settle at the bottom of the box. I suggest daily scoopings of poop and changing the litter completely every three to five days before the bottom becomes muddy. You can help keep odor under control by sprinkling a layer of baking soda under the litter, and you can keep the entire box drier by mixing the wet litter with the dry each day.

Specialty litters are available for different health conditions and situations. One litter helps control respiratory disease through a low-dust hypoallergenic formula; another, geared for seniors, is designed to keep the genital area clean and prevent urinary tract infection; and another, made for longhaired cats, does not adhere to kitty's coat. Also available are kitten training litters and a product with an attractant for cats who are reluctant to use the box. Natural, chemical-free litters are also offered. You'll find litters made from wheat, corn, or pine, and litters composed of recycled materials, such as newspaper and wood scraps. Browse through your pet store to check out the great variety, and in most cases, your cat will use what you choose. If you decide to change the litter you are currently buying, make the transition gradually, mixing the old and new litters for a few days before switching over entirely. Your cat will need time to get used to the feel and smell of the new product.

I made a recent house call to care for Biscuit, a sweet gray tabby whose owner had obviously not scooped out the box in many days. She uses clumping litter, which normally makes cleaning easier on a daily basis, but when I looked at the box I was horrified. There were several large piles of kitty poop and a boulder-size mound of reeking urine-soaked litter that took up nearly the entire box. Biscuit was such a good boy that he was still using the box, but many cats would not. They would, understandably, find another place to go.

I immediately dumped the litter out and washed the box thoroughly with diluted bleach, which I prefer to ammonia. Cat urine has ammonia in it, and cleaning with this substance adds to the overall smell. Once the box was washed, dried, and refreshed with new litter, Biscuit was once again a happy cat, at least on my watch. I made sure he had a few extra treats, as well.

Although many cat owners swear by plastic litter box liners, I am not a big fan. It is natural for cats to dig deep and bury their business. This digging often puts holes in the liners, allowing the urine and litter to soak through to the bottom of the box. This defeats the purpose of the liners and can make for quite a smelly mess—one that will not be appealing to you or your cat. Liners can also tear when you're cleaning out the box, so if you decide to employ them, you might try using two at a time.

If you prefer to use eco-friendly products, you can choose a litter that's made from wheat, corn, pine, or a recycled material such as newspaper or wood scraps.

DISTINCTIVE FELINE
NERO USES THE "LOO"

I remember a client who lived in Sutton Place, a swanky part of town. She had a very smart Siamese named Nero. When I first began caring for Nero, I was in the kitchen getting his food ready and thought I heard water running in the bathroom. I had just been there cleaning and changing his litter box, and I was sure I hadn't left the faucet on. I went to investigate and to my surprise, there was Nero straddling the toilet bowl, doing his business. I had never seen anything like it and could not help but laugh. Nero looked slightly embarrassed but finished and leapt off the bowl, completely ignoring his box. Even funnier, when I told his owner about it, she was shocked. She had often wondered why the litter box never seemed too dirty; now we knew. Nero had somehow taught himself to use the toilet.

Lessons from Nero

There is no end to what our feline friends can learn to do when they put their minds to it—including coming to terms with the litter box. Sometimes they will really throw you for a loop.

LITTER BOX TIPS

Cats are super easy to potty train. As kittens, they learn to use the litter box by watching their mothers or simply by being placed in one. Digging in litter and burying their waste is instinctive. This is why it's usually not difficult to set up and maintain a litter box that makes both you and your cat happy. These tips should help.

- Size matters, so choose a box that's right for your cat's age and health. Kittens and geriatric cats need boxes with lower sides, whereas healthy adult cats need room to turn around and are able to navigate higher sides that can help prevent scatter.

- Place the litter box in a quiet area that is not near your cat's food. Cats do not want to eat near the bathroom any more than we do.

- Try different litters until you find one that is acceptable to your cat. If she likes the litter, she'll be more likely to do her business inside the box. Don't switch the litter afterward unless there's a problem.

- Keep it clean! Scoop out the box daily, and change non-clumping litter every three to five days, and clumping litter every seven to ten days. Keep a small dust pan and brush by the box to help in daily cleanup. I have seen cats that I care for wait patiently while I clean out a box and then leap in to enjoy a fresh new bathroom. I can almost hear them say, "Ah . . . !"

- Make sure to check your Sunday paper circulars for cat litter coupons, and ask your friends who do not have cats to save them for you. It's a great way to save a few dollars on the essentials.

Never place your cat's litter box near her food. Just like you, your cat doesn't want to eat near her bathroom.

Minnie and Sam's High-Rise Bathroom

Minnie and Sam were two tabbies who lived in a lovely high-rise apartment with a terrace. I almost had a heart attack the first time I arrived to care for them. Their owner kept the litter box outside on the unenclosed, unprotected terrace. I asked him to please bring the box in for safety reasons. Fortunately, he agreed and from then on, the cats were able to use the "loo" without fear of accidentally falling down twenty stories!

If you notice your cat having problems in the litter box—if he appears to be straining, produces an excessive amount of urine, or has diarrhea—take him promptly to the vet. Remember the human/feline time line as told to me by a vet: If your cat has diarrhea for two days, it is equivalent to two weeks in human time—not a pleasant or healthy prospect. It's best to address these problems before the condition becomes more serious.

WHEN KITTY STOPS USING THE LITTER BOX

If you want your cat to keep using her litter box, keep it clean! Scoop the box daily and, depending on your choice of litter, replace it every three to seven days.

In my years as a cat sitter, I have seen a lot of bathroom-related problems, and feel I have been able to help many of my clients solve them. One cat, Bo, suddenly started using the couch as a litter box even though there were two hooded boxes in the same room. Understandably upset, my client put a plastic tarp over the couch to protect it and, hopefully, prevent him from using it. Unfortunately, it did not dissuade him. Bo's owner even tried repellents, which didn't work either.

I thought that since Bo was a senior, he might be getting pickier about his toilet. Perhaps he didn't like being in a hooded box anymore, and maybe the clumping litter was no longer to his liking. Cats really do have opinions, especially our special seniors. Anyway, I suggested taking the hood off one of the litter boxes and at the same time trying a different type of litter. I was so happy when my client called to say that these changes seemed to be working, but that she would temporarily leave the protective covering on the couch—just in case.

Recognize that avoidance of the litter box can be caused by a serious health disorder such as bladder or urinary tract infection, diabetes, thyroid dysfunction, GI problems, arthritis, or obesity. So if your cat suddenly stops using her box, it's important to take her to the veterinarian right away. Once the problem is diagnosed and treated, kitty's bathroom habits will probably return to normal.

If health problems have been ruled out, but your cat is still thinking outside the box, the following tips may help you get his litter box routine back to normal.

- Check the condition of the litter box itself. It's a good idea to replace it every year, since odor and bacteria can seep into the scratches made by digging. Cats have very sensitive noses and may avoid a box that smells offensive even when the litter is clean. Also make sure that the box size works for your cat and that you are providing

Boris Prefers Two Bathrooms

Boris is a wonderful cat with bad aim. Try as he might, he missed the litter box 90 percent of the time, driving his poor owner crazy. Even a box with a covered hood did not help—he was spooked by it. Finally, his owner had success with two boxes placed side by side in a secluded corner. I think the privacy and the extra space did the trick for Boris, who was not a one-size-fits-all kitty.

If you have multiple cats, offer multiple boxes. One box per cat is about right.

the right number of boxes for your family of felines. (See page 54 for more tips on choosing a litter box.)

🐾 Try a new litter, but make the change slowly. Mix some old litter with the new for a while, and then use just the new. (See page 55 for more tips on choosing litter.)

🐾 If your cat continues to use another part of the house as a bathroom, temporarily place an additional box in that exact spot. It might sound inconvenient, but your goal is to retrain your cat to use the litter box again—any litter box. When he begins using the new box, you can start moving it closer to the original box. Hopefully, once the new one is side by side with the old one, the problem will be solved.

🐾 If your cat is soiling another part of the house, clean the soiled area thoroughly with an enzymatic cleaner designed to remove the urine's scent, and put a food dish there for a few days. As a rule, cats will not go to the bathroom near their food. You can also try spraying the area with a product that replicates a cat's facial pheromones. Cats will not eliminate on anything they've marked with their scent.

- If your cat is urinating on a rug or mat, check the backing. I believe rubber backing emits an odor that, when washed, entices some cats to urinate. Try mats without rubber backings.

- If the problem seems to be your cat's aim and not total avoidance of the box, place a plastic mat or puppy training pad by the entrance to the litter box to help catch the occasional accident and make the area cleaner. A litter box fitted with a large hood can have the same helpful effect.

Patience and perseverance will go a long way in solving litter box problems. Cats by nature have meticulous bathroom habits, so if you provide enough clean litter boxes, place them in locations where your cat is comfortable, and take your cat to the vet at the first sign of trouble, both your nose and your cat will appreciate the results.

Feline Fact

Although cats use both paws for some tasks, like humans, they prefer one paw over the other in certain situations. Most male cats are southpaws—they use their left front paws for all those one-pawed jobs, like pulling tuna out of a can.

Health Care

O ur feline friends ask so little from us. Mostly, they want love, attention, and, of course, food. In return, they give us unconditional love and companionship. They can even lower our blood pressure, which contributes to our health and longevity. Our kitties can enjoy long, healthy lives, too, if we nurture them, keep them indoors, and partner with our veterinarians to prevent health problems and treat them promptly when they do occur.

Cats are very good at hiding illnesses, but they can be just as miserable as we are when they are sick. Throughout my work as a cat sitter, I have always advised clients to pay close attention when their cat's habits change, as this is a good indicator of a potential problem. If your kitty starts behaving differently—if he loses his appetite, develops bad litter box habits, starts hiding from you, or exhibits extreme lethargy, for instance—it could be a sign of illness.

Over the years, I have been asked to give pills and other medicine to many of the cats I care for. I remember one client told me she would be going on vacation and her kitty, Marina, needed half a pill each day. She asked if I would mind giving it to her, quickly adding that it was very easy. Of course it was easy—her husband restrained Marina while she pilled her! I laughed and told my client that if her husband would stay home to help, there would be no problem. Naturally, that didn't happen, and off they went, leaving me to figure out the best way to give Marina her meds. It didn't help that she was very shy.

Luckily, Marina was a true princess and loved being brushed. It sounds ridiculous, but I would sit on the living room floor, wave the brush, and call out, "Marina, brushies!" and she would appear. I would have the pill ready in one hand while brushing her with the other. I'd wait for just the right moment when she was the most relaxed and quickly pop the pill in her mouth—and I never missed a brush stroke!"

Once diagnosed, it can be hard to persuade your cat that any medicine will make her feel better. Still, you have to do what's best for her even when it causes some short-term annoyance or discomfort—both hers and yours. This chapter provides guidelines and tips that will enable you to safeguard your feline friend's health and well-being throughout her lifetime.

Cats are stoics by nature and will hide their illness. This is why it's so important for you to be alert to any changes in your cat's behavior.

GETTING PROPER MEDICAL CARE FOR YOUR CAT

We all want our kitties to be safe and healthy, and the best way to do that is to make sure they enjoy a good diet, get plenty of TLC, and, just as important, get regular checkups and all their vaccinations. Whether you suspect a health problem or not, I urge you to take your cat for a checkup every year, and your senior cat twice a year. Better to be safe than sorry. Annual veterinary visits make it easier and less expensive to treat health problems and can sometimes even prevent them. Your first step, of course, is to find a vet who is right for you and your kitty.

Even if your cat seems free of health problems, make sure he has a checkup every year. If your kitty is a senior, twice a year is even better.

Finding the Right Veterinarian

Can you believe I once knew a vet who was allergic to cats? How is that for choosing a career? He managed by wearing gloves when he saw patients. This system worked until he met Felix, a large tuxedo cat with an observant eye. Felix took one look at those gloves and totally freaked out. He ended up on top of the vet's head! No joke. The vet and Felix lived to tell the tale, but I still laugh when I think about it.

One of the best ways to find a vet is to ask another cat owner or a trusted cat sitter for a referral. We see and hear it all, believe me. Visit the office and make sure that the chemistry is right with the vet; this is just as vital as having the right chemistry with your regular doctor. Also consider other aspects of his practice. Is the staff polite and responsive? Do they show concern for you and your cat? For me, this is

The best way to find a
good veterinarian is to
ask another cat owner
or a cat sitter. Your
local animal shelter or
rescue organization
may also be able to
make a referral.

important. I also like a practice with several vets; there is always someone available for consultation. Above all, have faith in your own judg-
ment. You would not entrust the care of your child to someone you are
unsure about. The same is true of your cat.

Some people use cat-only vets who specialize in cat-specific health
issues, but I recommend finding the best vet for you and your feline
friend. Depending on your needs, you also might want to look for a vet
who makes house calls, especially if you have a large family of pets or
your kitty gets frantic at the sight of a carrier. You can find a cat vet in
your area by visiting the American Association of Feline Practitioners'
website at www.catvets.com.

Knowing When to Contact Your Vet

Please take your cat to the vet immediately if he stops eating, drools,
strains to urinate or defecate, has diarrhea or constipation for more
than twenty-four hours, is not using the litter box, is extremely thirsty
or produces excessive amounts of urine, is hiding more than usual,
coughs or vomits chronically, is losing weight, or becomes aggressive.
While you're at the office, make sure he is current on his vaccinations.
The FVRCP vaccine (feline rhinotracheitis, calicivirus, and panleukope-
nia) protects your cat against feline herpes, calicivirus, and distemper.
In addition, your cat needs to be protected against rabies. These vac-
cines are considered necessary for *all* cats, including those who live indoors. If your kitty is allowed to go outdoors, which I do not
recommend, he should also be vaccinated against feline leukemia virus
(FeLV) and feline immunodeficiency virus (FIV). Since urgent health

situations can occur when your vet's office is closed, make sure you know the name and location of a good emergency clinic in your area. Your veterinarian should be able to refer you to a reliable facility.

Giving Your Cat Medication

Medicating cats can be challenging, as any cat owner knows. You should have your vet show you the proper way to administer meds and follow all directions. Be sure to ask if they should be stored in the refrigerator. If left out, they could go bad and make kitty worse.

When given the choice, I prefer pills over liquid medicine. Liquids can be messy and get all over you and your cat. Cats can also spit out the liquid or drool so much that most of it ends up on the floor. I suggest the direct approach, but try not to make a big show out of it. Instead of wrapping your cat in a towel for what I call the "mummy maneuver," sit next to him, pet him calmly and quietly, and then, putting slight pressure at the corners of his mouth with your thumb and middle finger to get him to open up, insert the pill. If you are using a liquid, it is usually dispensed in an eyedropper. I prefer to use a needle-less syringe, which your vet will be happy to provide. It's faster and easier to use. You might also ask if liquid medicine can be flavored to taste like tuna or chicken. This can make the situation much more pleasant for your kitty.

To give pills to a wary cat, wait until she is hungry, and try crushing the pill in some baby food or a tiny amount of tuna. There is also a wonderful product that allows you to place a pill in the center pocket of a yummy pea-sized food treat. I have recommended this many times to

Try placing pills in special food treats designed with pill-sized pockets. Many cats don't even realize that they're taking meds when these yummy treats are used.

clients and have used it myself. It's terrific—the feline version of a spoonful of sugar helping the medicine go down.

I had to give one of my feline charges, Alice, a pill for her heart condition. Naturally I didn't want to get the little kitty upset by what I knew would be a daily occurrence. I talked it over with her owner and suggested cat treats that hold pills. Thank goodness, Alice liked it so much she would even come out of hiding to have her treat.

If you find it difficult to medicate your cat, ask your vet if you can get the medication in the form of a flavored liquid, a flavored treat, or a transdermal gel that can be rubbed on the inside of the ear.

Some owners find it difficult or impossible to give their cats pills or liquid medications, which can become a big problem when kitty needs to be treated for a chronic condition. If you are challenged by a resistant feline, talk over the options with your vet. Some medications are available as flavored chews, which can be presented as treats. In some cases, there is also the alternative of transdermal gel medications, which are rubbed on the inside of the cat's ear and absorbed through the skin. These meds, though pricy, are easy to apply and can be a real life saver. Just make sure to wear a rubber glove or finger cot during application so that you don't absorb the medication along with your cat.

For some conditions, injections are necessary. If your doctor finds that your kitty requires injections, don't panic. Many owners, once trained by a vet or vet technician, find it much easier to administer a shot than to pill a cat. Medications like insulin are given in the scruff of the neck with a tiny needle, and cats are often unaware that the injection is taking place. Have your vet demonstrate the proper procedure and answer all your questions before you do it on your own. Also be aware that the Internet makes available instructional videos of veterinarians administering injections as well as other forms of medication. This will allow you to watch the procedure as often as necessary in the comfort of your home.

GROOMING YOUR CAT

A well-groomed cat is a happy cat, and you can help with daily brushing and regular nail clipping. Very often when I brush my kitties, they get in the mood to clean up and start licking their paws. Nail clipping is important as well. Not only will it save your furniture, but nails that grow too long can get caught in carpets and rugs, making it difficult for your cat to get around.

Just as when you're giving medicine, you should not turn brushing or nail trimming into a huge, scary issue that frightens your cat. If you stay calm and relaxed, your kitty will not be stressed.

Brushing Your Cat

Although cats are terrific self-groomers, I always feel you should help them with a daily brushing. It is a wonderful bonding experience and helps control excess cat hair and prevent hairballs, dry skin, and dandruff. A good daily brushing is especially important for longhaired kitties, as long fur can form mats that pull painfully on skin and eventually lead to infection.

I have a client who has taken an extreme but effective approach to ensuring that her longhaired cats are mat-free. She has a professional groomer give Ollie and Sasha "lion cuts" several times a year. Their body hair is closely cropped, but their heads, legs, and the ends of their tails are left fluffy. It is adorable, though I am not sure how the cats feel about it.

When brushing cats—my own or my charges—I like to use a soft wire slicker brush, which has lots of tiny wires to untangle matted and snarled fur. I even give these brushes to my clients as presents. Some vets recommend flea combs even in the absence of fleas. The fine, closely spaced metal teeth are good at removing dead hair. For long-haired cats, you might want to try a deshedding comb, which grooms the undercoat and topcoat at the same time. When the brushing session is over, I sometimes dampen my hand and gently pet my kitties to pick up any loose hair that remains on the surface. They like the sensation, and hair that could end up on my clothes or in their stomachs goes into the trash instead.

Cats tend to shed more in the summer months, so extra brushing is generally required during that season. In the winter, central heating can dry out their coats, causing not only shedding but also flaking skin. I suggest that you occasionally add "cat-approved" oils, available in pet

Brushing your cat is beneficial in a number of ways. It prevents painful matting, helps avoid the formation of hairballs, and acts as a relaxing kitty massage.

Ronnie Loves the Brush

Ronnie, with his luxuriant orange and white coat, was one of those cats who loves a good brushing. Whenever I would care for Ronnie, he let it be known that brushing came first. I would sit next to him on the floor while he rolled from side to side to make sure I didn't miss a spot. I used to tell his owners that I could make a pillow out of Ronnie's hair.

stores, to their food during the colder months. You will find that a little maintenance goes a long way.

Most cats really enjoy being brushed, but there are those who do not. Fern, a very prim and proper kitty I care for, allows me to complete only a few quick swipes with the brush. She then shoots me a look to let me know that she has endured a terrible violation. It's best to approach cats like this when they are relaxing or even sleeping. Be calm and try not to wake them up. They will let you know when enough is enough. For those really difficult cases, consider using a professional groomer. Some even make house calls. I like to give my cats a treat after each session. This way they know that when the brush comes out, a treat will soon follow.

If your cat doesn't like to be brushed, try to approach her when she's sleeping, and stop when she's had enough. By providing a treat after each session, you will help kitty associate brushing with a pleasurable reward.

Cleaning Up Cat Hair

I am asked about cat hair issues all the time, and for most cat owners, removing excess cat hair from the house is as big a concern as removing it from their cat. Fur looks great on your kitty but not on your clothes. There is nothing quite like sitting down on your couch while wearing a nice pair of black pants, only to pick up a mountain of hair when you stand up.

I once had to go directly to a special dinner after a cat-sitting visit in my neighborhood. There I was in my dinner clothes, wondering how I was going to avoid getting hair all over myself, particularly since my very affectionate furry charges, Annie and Phoebe, loved to greet me with welcoming rubs. Anyway, I rolled up the legs of my pantsuit before entering their apartment—luckily, no one was in the hallway to see me—and must have been quite a sight dancing around, trying to avoid two kitties who just wanted to share the love. I managed to complete my tasks of giving them food, fresh water, and litter without getting tons of hair on my good suit. Fortunately, the small lint roller I always carry with me took care of any stray hairs. I never leave home without my trusty lint roller!

Although it's especially important to provide daily brushings for longhaired cats, believe it or not, shorthaired kitties can make it harder to keep your home fur-free. Because their fur is closer to the skin, the undercoat has more body oil, which makes it cling stubbornly to furniture, carpets, and clothes—especially knitted fabrics and velvets.

When you have cats, it makes sense to keep certain things on hand to help "de-fur" your home and your belongings. In addition to a lint roller, both a damp sponge and masking tape are very good for cleaning hair off furniture and clothes. I also find the red Velcro-type lint brushes useful on napped and even smoother fabrics. They seem to last forever, too. If company is coming and you don't have time for a major cleanup, use a handheld vacuum for fast cat hair pickup. You can also find sheets of sticky tape at pet stores designed to pull cat hair off your furniture in one fell swoop. To help rid your carpets of hair, run a powerful upright vacuum on them every few days. Use the attachments to clean carpeted tree houses, pet beds, favorite couches, and other areas where pet hair can accumulate.

If you're thinking of renovating or redecorating your home, you may want to consider materials that are less prone to gather and hang onto fur. Wood and tile floors make it much easier to clean up cat hair, especially if you use a microfiber mop. Flat fabrics without nap or

To "de-fur" your home, you'll want to keep certain items on hand. A lint roller, a damp sponge, masking tape, and Velcro-type lint brushes are all useful. For superfast cleanups, use a handheld vacuum.

tufts are less "sticky" than napped fabrics and less likely to collect fur in the first place.

Clipping Your Cat's Nails

To trim your cat's nails, use nail clippers specifically designed for cats. Because a cat's nails are round, human nail clippers can crush their claws. Pet stores usually carry two styles of clippers—a scissor style and a so-called guillotine style—so you can pick the one that seems most comfortable to handle. A vet or groomer will also be glad to steer you to an effective, easy-to-use device.

To adequately see your cat's claws, vertically press the pad of each toe between your thumb and forefinger. Be gentle, because cats' paws are sensitive. Look for the *quick*—the pink blood vessel in the nail—and clip below it (in other words, closer to the tip of the nail). If you cut the quick, it will bleed and cause pain. Always have some styptic powder on hand to stop the bleeding just in case, but you won't have that problem if you cut off only the tip of the nail. You may want to select clippers that detect the quick and light up red where it's not safe to clip, and green where it is safe to clip.

If you start handling your cat's paws when he's a kitten, he will be accustomed to it, and grooming will not turn into a battle. Be sure to reward your kitty with a treat, favorite toy, praise, or lots of affection afterward, so he will actually look forward to the routine. If your cat really puts up a fuss or you just don't trust yourself to do it, take him to a professional groomer. Some groomers make house calls, and some shelters will do free nail trimmings for cats they adopted out.

To trim your cat's claws, use a trimmer that's specifically designed for cats. Human nail clippers can crush kitty's claws.

Feline Fact

Each of a cat's front paws has a dew claw, which is raised above the ground on the inside of the leg. In the wild, cats use this claw to hold down their prey.

CARING FOR CATS WITH SPECIAL NEEDS

Cats come in many shapes and sizes—and each is adorable in my book. Just like humans, cats have different needs at each stage of life and require different amounts and types of attention. Although you might think that kitties with disabilities would be difficult to care for, with a little extra consideration and some simple strategies, these special felines can live long and happy lives.

Kittens

Years ago, I rescued two kittens from a construction site. I immediately took them to the vet, who said they were about seven weeks old and seemed in good health. She gave them their first series of vaccinations and took blood and fecal tests. Fortunately, Roscoe and Bandit, as I named them, were old enough to start on kitten food.

Because I had other cats, I kept my new charges confined to my bedroom until all the test results were back. This arrangement also allowed me to keep track of how much they were eating, how much they were urinating, and their bowel movements. I purchased a small litter box with low sides and added a half-inch of unscented clay litter—just enough for burying. The cuties immediately climbed in the box and did what comes naturally. I was careful to wash out the box every few days with hot water and a mild kitten-safe cleaner, which I got at a pet store. I also bought them a sisal scratching post to start them scratching on the right surface—not furniture!—and a few little toys with bells to chase. Every time they used the post, which was a lot, the kittens received a

If you adopt a kitten, make sure to scale things down for your new baby. Place the food in small, shallow dishes, and choose a litter box with low sides.

food treat. In my experience, kittens usually don't appreciate catnip until they are about four to five months old.

When Roscoe and Bandit got a clean bill of health, I opened the bedroom door and out they scampered. Greeting them was my eight-year-old cat, Muriel, who immediately adopted them and proceeded to give them a good bath. Even though they are now double her size, she still mothers them. They are a wonderful addition to my furry family.

Kittens are not a lot of trouble—in fact, they're a joy—but you do want to give them age-appropriate food and make sure that they have a scaled-down litter box that's right for their size. You also want to start forming good feline habits right away. That's why toys and a scratching post are so important.

Just as you would childproof your home to prepare for a baby, you also need to kittenproof your home to keep baby kitties safe. Look around for objects they can swallow, climb into, or get stuck in, and make them inaccessible to your little ones. Keep trash cans closed and toilet lids down. Always check reclining chairs before closing, and check dishwashers, clothes dryers, and washing machines before starting. Keep harmful chemicals out of their reach. Kittens have a lot of energy and are curious, so you'll also want to keep breakable objects out of the way. Then enjoy the show, because there's nothing more fun than kittens acting like kittens.

Seniors

For many years I looked after two elderly Siamese cats, Jade (age twenty) and Pearl (age twenty-one). When I arrived, they would be

Feline Fact
Mature cats sleep
about eighteen hours
a day. Yet cats move
from the sleep state to
full alertness faster
than any other animal
in the world.

sleeping in their favorite spot and I'd gently wake them up so they wouldn't be startled. They would then slowly follow me into the kitchen where I would prepare their food. Their owners, with approval from the veterinarian, boiled chicken with juices, ground it up in a blender, and wrapped up individual meals for them. They also had varieties of baby food, but no dry food at all. I think Jade and Pearl were gumming their meals by then. They would eat what they wanted and slowly walk back to their spot to continue their snooze. I chuckle when I think about what I would always whisper to both, "Please be okay until your parents get home." Their owners laughed politely when I told them about my fears. I guess they thought that Jade and Pearl would go on forever.

I remember a time when an eight-year-old cat was considered a senior. With more nutritious food and better medical care, cats age fifteen and up are no longer uncommon. If one of your cats is a senior, keep in mind that aging is a natural process, but that you can make your kitty's quality of life better and help her live longer by meeting her special needs.

Gretel Aims High

Gretel was a rambunctious kitty who loved jumping up on everything. As she aged, she got arthritis and slowed down considerably, but still wanted to jump up to her favorite places—particularly a certain window that overlooked a lovely street. Her owner constructed a special set of cat stairs so that the increasingly frail Gretel could always get to "her" window.

First, stay on top of any changes in your cat and report them to your veterinarian. She may be able to provide medications or suggest a different food that will help manage health problems and make your kitty more comfortable.

Cats do get arthritis as they age, and that will slow them down. To help your cat climb up onto a bed, sofa, or windowsill for bird-watching, a carpeted ramp or pet stair climber will come in handy and provide some exercise for aching joints. You don't want your kitty to get depressed because she can no longer reach her favorite spots, including all those warm, sunny areas that cats love so much.

Check with your vet for guidance in choosing the appropriate senior diet for your furry companion; there are many varieties. Make sure she has fresh water every day, and try putting an ice cube in her water bowl. She might like to play with it as it melts. If your cat has difficulty bending down to eat, place her food on a raised platform. Pet stores sell raised feeding stations plus automatic feeders with timers for seniors who now prefer eating several small meals a day.

If your older kitty is starting to miss the litter box, put a few extra boxes with low sides in the house. Puppy training pads placed around the litter box are great for catching anything that doesn't quite make it into the litter.

Some seniors develop poor eyesight and become disoriented when they roam around at night. To help your kitty out, place a night-light or two in strategic areas of your home.

Senior cats need extra help with grooming. Consider keeping on hand waterless shampoos in case kitty gets into something messy, and pet wipes, which are useful for cleaning hard-to-reach hind areas.

Be aware that as your cat gets older, she may need you to make some changes in her environment. A carpeted ramp or pet stair climber can help your elder kitty enjoy all her favorite perches and sunning spots.

Bert and Murphy Bond

Older cats and seniors are a great match. One of my clients dropped off her cat, Mikey, with her seventy-two-year-old Uncle Bert so he could care for the kitty while she was away. They got along great. In fact, when Mikey returned home, Bert missed his new friend so much that he ended up adopting a ten-year-old cat named Murphy. He says that having Murphy to look after has brought great joy into his life and has made it much less lonely.

Don't stop playing with your senior cat. Even if kitty has arthritis, a daily play session can be beneficial to his mental and physical health.

Don't forget to incorporate exercise into your kitty's day. This is especially important for cats with arthritis. A fishing pole toy is fun, or try throwing small treats across the room for her to chase—that is a favorite game in my house. It is also important to brush seniors daily. This helps rid them of loose hair that can be ingested and become hairballs, and also stimulates their coat. Brushing doubles as a gentle massage, which is a great way to spend quality time together.

One last note: A senior cat can be a calm, affectionate, and wonderful companion. I have often said that senior cats and senior people can be a winning combination, so if there is a cat lover in your family who is thinking of adopting for companionship, consider an elder kitty.

Cats With Disabilities

I care for a deaf cat named Sweetie who truly is a sweetie. I have seen many deaf cats manage very well by making use of their other senses—

even some who have learned to respond to hand signals. Sweetie certainly does. I wave and he runs right over to me, particularly when I turn on the TV. We both like to watch the game shows, although I don't let him near the remote.

If you have a deaf cat, or any cat with special needs, keep him indoors, where you can control his environment. Take the time to be careful, practice common sense, and make sure all family members show equal consideration for your kitty. I am sure you will find it a rewarding experience.

If your cat has a disability such as deafness, keep her indoors so that you can better control her environment.

Blind cats adapt surprisingly well to their environment. If the blindness is sudden—if it's the result of an accident or illness, for instance—you may want to pad the legs of your furniture until your kitty learns his way around. Just be sure to avoid moving the furniture, food bowls, or litter. Consistency is the key.

Even cats with neurological problems can adapt and thrive. I cared for an Abyssinian who had a stroke when he was twenty years old. He

Baby Wins the Day!

Baby was born with a neurological condition that inhibits his balance and prevents him from walking properly. However, his strength and determination have helped him overcome this disability, and he is definitely the "top cat" in a household that includes three other felines who are able-bodied. Baby is unable to walk without falling over, and he gets around by starting off at a run, which seems to keep the kitty on his feet and land him at his destination in record time.

DISTINCTIVE FELINE
REGGIE—SAYING GOODBYE

 Reggie was a people cat. He loved nothing more than to be petted and brushed. When I visited, he would follow me around and seemed very in tune with his human companion. His owners could not help but adore him.

One night in his later years, Reggie broke his routine by walking into the office of his owner, who was working very late. Reggie sat right by him until he finally finished his task and went off to bed. All cats are creatures of habit, and the owner remembers noting how unusual Reggie's nocturnal visit was. The next morning, he and his wife found Reggie lying on the floor next to their bed. He had peacefully passed away in his sleep. Both of them were upset, and so was I, but they were convinced that with his office visit, Reggie had said goodbye.

Lessons from Reggie

A cat's love can be deep and unconditional. Sharing your life with one will only enhance it. Unfortunately, they are not with us as long as we would like, so please enjoy them while they are here. I have owned many cats, and each has been a joy. However, when one passes it is very painful. I know they are with their other furry friends in a place where treats and playtime are everlasting.

lost his balance on one side and couldn't climb into a litter box. So I made one for him by using a large rectangular aluminum baking pan and cutting off one end so he could walk into it without climbing. It worked really well. It still had high sides and was big enough so that he could turn around. I also raised his food and water bowls because he had difficulty bending his head. His owner and I decided to keep him confined to the den so he wouldn't wander around and get into difficult situations.

My charges Faith and Hope have had neurological problems since birth. They have difficulty getting up and walking, and they stagger and wobble on their feet. The whole apartment is set up for their safety. Carpeting keeps them from slipping. The bed is low to the floor, so it's easy for them to climb up, since they can't jump. Fortunately, they are able to get into their two litter boxes—and they never miss. Because their heads shake while they're eating, they are fed on flat plates so that they don't hit the sides of their faces, which would happen if they ate from bowls. They're sloppy eaters and splatter food, but they gobble up whatever falls on the floor. Despite their disability, they are happy and beautiful girls. I have found that to be the case with all cats whom we might label *disabled.* That word means nothing to them, and they don't seem to love life any less because of their challenges.

Health care is a key part of sharing life with a kitty. Be observant of your cat's behavior and keep in mind that even a small change may signal trouble. A little time, thought, and care can go a long way in giving your cat a happy, healthy life.

Feline Fact

A cat uses his whiskers to measure distance and determine if he can fit through an opening. Cats' whiskers are so ultra-sensitive that they can detect the slightest change in the direction of a breeze.

When Kitty Misbehaves

Cats do all sorts of things that delight us; that is one of the reasons we love them. They also do things that we don't like, don't understand, or both. Often, what we might think is a behavioral problem could be a medical issue or part of a cat's natural instinct. Cats need to know that their territory is safe from predators and that they can count on a secure place to eat, sleep, and do their business. What they do may seem strange or destructive to you, but it is an expression of their nature.

I have encountered many types of cats in my time as a cat sitter, and Rocky was a good example of how some do not always "roll with the punches" of life. I had cared for Rocky, a handsome gray cat, for many years. He was friendly and especially appreciative of the catnip treats I would bring him. He was also very pampered and had grown dependent on his owner, who was home most of the time.

Then, as I learned on one fateful visit, Rocky's personality took a sad and dangerous turn. After I entered the apartment, the usually complacent Rocky arched his back and growled at me. I was immediately concerned, but no amount of cooing would calm him. He became more aggressive and lunged at my leg, actually drawing blood.

Shocked, I quickly took care of his needs and left in a hurry. On several subsequent occasions, I hoped to find that Rocky had returned to his old self. Sadly, he hadn't. I later learned that his owner had a new boyfriend and was spending very little time at home. I am convinced Rocky had gotten very jealous and was acting out, not with my client, but with me. It's a shame, but he couldn't cope with having a rival.

If your sweet and friendly cat suddenly becomes aggressive, first consider if his behavior may have been triggered by a significant change in your household. If not, he might be sick or in pain. Please take him to the vet right away to determine if he has any medical issues. Hopefully, they can be resolved.

Fortunately, when most cats misbehave, their conduct is a little less extreme than Rocky's. Here are suggestions to help you with some of the more challenging behaviors in which our kitties engage.

Cats don't mean to be destructive when they scratch your furniture. They scratch to stretch their bodies, to remove the dead sheaths from their claws, to mark their territory, and sometimes, just to play.

SCRATCHING FURNITURE

Scratching is a natural part of a cat's routine and a nice way for cats to relieve stress and stretch their muscles. It also allows them to mark their territory through the scent glands in their paws. The good news is that there are strategies that can help you save your precious furniture from kitty's damaging claws. The following story is a bit extreme, but it shows an approach that worked for one family.

I used to care for a bright orange-and-white cat named Reggie, who was as gentle as a lamb and very friendly. Reggie's owners were well-off and lived in a beautiful Manhattan apartment on Park Avenue filled with expensive furniture. They adored Reggie, and the first time I visited the apart-  ment to care for him, I couldn't help but laugh. He had chosen one chair out of a very pricy Louis XVI dining room set as his personal scratching post. The chair was completely shredded and had all the stuffing torn out of it. Meanwhile, the rest of the gorgeous chairs in the beautiful dining room were untouched. When I asked his owners about it, they told me that they would rather have Reggie destroy one chair than scratch his way through the entire set, so they never scolded him for work-ing on "his" chair.

If your cat is damaging your couch or chair, the first thing you should do is invest in a good scratching post that is at least three feet high—large enough for a nice stretch. The material covering the post should be a tight weave like commercial carpeting or sisal. Place the post by the furniture currently being scratched, and bring your kitty there several times a day. Hold

Place your cat's scratching post next to the furniture she has been damaging. To make the post more inviting, rub it with some dried catnip. If you have the room, invest in a tall cat tree house that will serve as both a post and a perch.

her paws up, imitating a scratch, and show her how much more fun it is than your new couch. To make the post even more enticing, rub it with a good dose of catnip—a great motivator—and refresh it weekly to keep your cat interested. I also recommend carpeted tree houses that are four or five feet tall if you have the room. This way, your kitty will be able to scratch and climb, two things cats love to do. Make sure you reward her with praise, affection, or treats whenever she uses her own furniture rather than yours.

If your furry friend just can't keep her claws off your favorite chairs, place double-sided adhesive tape on her target areas. Cats do not like the sensation of tape. Pet stores sell double-sided tape in sheets and various sizes for this purpose.

Although you may not love the look, another option is to cover your furniture with a throw made of denim fabric. Denim is pretty rugged, and I have found that cats are usually not attracted to it.

Sometimes, no matter what you do, your kitty will still indulge in scratching his favorite piece of furniture. To minimize the damage, I

Feline Fact

Cats have scent glands on the underside of their front paws, on either side of their head, on their lips, and at the base of their tail. When they scratch or rub against an object—or against you—they are marking their territory.

Larry and Moe Start Their Engines

A carpeted tree house is great for diverting your kitty's attention away from scratching the furniture. Some cats, though, take it to the next level. Larry and Moe love nothing more than chasing each other up and down the tree house in their home. They go racing around the living room, through the kitchen, up and down the tree house, and back again. It's always the Indy 500 in their home, but at least the furniture is safe.

suggest clipping his nails about every two weeks. Turn to page 75 of Chapter 5 for more information on this important aspect of your cat's grooming routine.

HOUSEHOLD ACCIDENTS

We know that cats are very clean animals, but there are always those little accidents no one can predict or control. It's all part of sharing space with our feline friends.

If your cat starts using another part of the house as a litter box or simply "misses" the box, there is a lot you can do to get kitty back to normal bathroom habits. (Turn to page 60 in Chapter 4 for time-proven tips.) Of course, these mishaps are not always behavioral issues. In fact, they can be a sign of a medical condition such as a bladder or urinary tract infection. So if your kitty frequently misses the box or soils the house in any other way, it's important to take him to the veterinarian to rule out medical causes.

When I make my house calls, I always keep my fingers crossed that I won't find an "accident" on a rug or nicely upholstered furniture— but in all these years of caring for cats, I have found plenty. I remember when one of my well-to-do clients on the Upper West Side of Manhattan had just installed a new beige wall-to-wall carpet. Her cats, Sparky and Cosmo, were as cute as could be. Of course, on my first visit after the rug was installed, I was greeted by a huge hairball surrounded by Sparky or Cosmo's morning meal. Neither would claim responsibility, but since they both seemed fine, I wasn't worried about them. Besides, passing a hairball probably made them feel better.

Daily brushings can help eliminate the excess hair that leads to hairballs. If more frequent grooming doesn't help, try hairball-control foods, treats, or pastes.

The carpet, however, needed attention. My client must have anticipated a moment like this because she had an excellent stain and odor remover on hand. So I went to work on the rug while Sparky and Cosmo sat close by to oversee the cleanup process.

As you learned in Chapter 5 (see page 71), you can help prevent hairballs with daily brushings, which reduce the amount of fur that is swallowed during self-grooming sessions. If hairballs persist, there are treats, pastes, and even special diets that can prevent or lessen their formation by moving the fur through the digestive system. These products are available in well-stocked pet stores and many supermarkets.

Whether it's a hairball, vomit, or litter box accident, you need to maintain a good supply of stain and odor removers, especially if you have carpets. Most of these products work well if the stain is new. Older stains can be more difficult to remove. When urine accidents occur, it's important to use an enzymatic cleaner that gets rid of odors as well as the stain. Eliminating the odor will prevent repeat soiling in that spot. There are many pet-safe stain removers on the market, but inexpensive, age-old products like white vinegar and club soda are also effective. For tough rug and fabric stains, ask for suggestions from your local carpet store or pet store.

A number of houseplants are toxic to cats to one degree or another. Some of the most common poisonous plants include Easter lilies, mistletoe, philodendron, and poinsettia.

EATING AND DIGGING UP HOUSEPLANTS

Cats are diggers by nature, and I am often asked how to stop them from digging in the wrong places, like your favorite indoor planters. This creates a mess for you and can put your kitty in danger because some plants are poisonous. Among the most common toxic plants are lilies, which can be fatal to your cat. For a complete list of toxic and nontoxic plants, visit the ASPCA website (http://www.aspca.org/pet-care/poison-control/plants/).

It is easier to try to cat-proof your plants rather than to enforce a "paws-off" approach. Younger cats seem to get into trouble a bit more than our older kitties, so it's best to move your houseplants out of harm's way, perhaps onto a high narrow shelf, if your cats are still at that playful age. Also try placing objects around the plants to block access. To deter digging, put smooth stones or crumpled aluminum foil on top of the soil, or sprinkle it with fresh orange peel, which should be changed regularly to keep it as aromatic as possible. (Some cats find a citrus scent offensive.) Pet stores sell repellents, but double-check with your vet to make sure that they are safe for your cat.

To further divert your cat's attention from your houseplants, cultivate a pot of kitty grass, which is sold in pet stores. When two of my wonderful kitties were four-month-old kittens, they used to snooze on top of a large flower box of kitty grass I planted for them. Little did I suspect that this would be so inviting, they would want to sleep on it instead of nibbling it. I have now planted the kitty grass in pots that are too small for napping and suitable only for nibbling. You can also add a catnip plant; just don't leave it out when you're not home or it might get pulled apart.

Some cats love to dig up the dirt in planters. To discourage this practice, try topping the soil with smooth stones, crumpled aluminum foil, or fresh orange peel. If your cats are young and playful, moving the plants to a high shelf may be the best option.

CHEWING, SHREDDING, AND LICKING

When one of my regular clients is traveling, she leaves any instructions for the care of her cat, Herbie, on the kitchen table along with my check.

When I arrived recently to care for him, I did not see either. After a quick search, I noticed shredded paper strewn across the kitchen floor. Herbie had obviously chewed the note and check to bits. Fortunately, this was not my first visit and all was well, but now, everything essential gets taped to a kitchen cabinet.

Some cats love to shred paper. It could be the texture or the crinkly noise it makes, or maybe they're just being mischievous—they don't know the difference between a check and a takeout menu! Be sure to file your receipts and provide toys that kitty can chew to her heart's content.

Cats are attracted to all sorts of objects, and they can pick the strangest things to chew or lick. One of my cats likes to lick my hair, which I do not encourage for many reasons—his and mine. I know another cat who likes to lick her owner's beard. In general, when your cats lick or groom either you or another household pet, it's a sign of affection, similar to the way a mother cat licks her kittens.

Plastic bags are a favorite with some cats because kitties can smell the rendered animal fat used to make the plastic. Eating plastic is dangerous because it can cause an intestinal obstruction. Please store these bags out of harm's way, and always check your floors for small objects such as needles, pins, rubber bands, and other small inedible items your cat might eat. Human medicine can be lethal to a cat, so please check floors and other surfaces for pills, too.

Cats with the condition known as *pica* crave and eat inedible substances such as plastic, wood, cloth, paper, the coating on photographs, and more. Eating these materials could be life-threatening, as they can be toxic or cause an obstruction. If your cat shows signs of pica, it's important to first take her to your veterinarian to determine if there is a medical cause for this behavior. Once a medical condition has been ruled out, talk with a feline behaviorist, who can explore psychological causes and recommend behavioral modification techniques. Please take your cat's penchant for eating inedible substances seriously and keep those objects out of her reach.

SLEEPING ISSUES

Many people enjoy sleeping with their cats, and I am one of them. Having a cat lying next to you or stretched out across you can provide a nice warm, fuzzy feeling. Not only do I have a few cats sharing space on the bed, but my dog, Ziggy, likes to snuggle with his favorite cat, Ethel. They are so cute together. Of course, once all my pets have claimed their spots and are sleeping peacefully, it's not an easy task to

If kitty's bedtime shenanigans prevent you from falling asleep, try engaging him in play right before you turn in. With any luck, he'll be ready for bed about the same time you are.

Muriel and Chester Go "Undercover"

I was asked to look after two adorable cats, Muriel and Chester, but was told only at the last minute that construction was being done in the apartment. When I arrived, I found the furniture piled in the living room with tarps thrown over everything and no cats in sight. I was horrified. Fortunately, when they heard my voice, Muriel and Chester came out from under the furniture. There was also a pet frog that was left in his container on the living room desk! If I hadn't removed the paint tarp, the poor little guy might have suffocated. I did advise my client that in the future, she should make better arrangements for her pets.

Feline Fact
A cat's hearing is far
more sensitive than
that of a human being
or even a dog. Cats
also have thirty-two
muscles that control
the outer ear, allowing
each ear to turn
independently and
home in on sounds.

get up in the middle of the night. When I return to bed, they have re-arranged themselves, leaving me a small space at the edge of the mattress. I don't really mind squeezing myself in, though. It's nice to know that my furry friends are safe, sound, and sleeping comfortably.

Most people find it helpful to create some boundaries for successful snoozing. If you are a light sleeper, try to establish a side of the bed for your cat. Put something soft like a piece of fleece or a bed pillow on the designated spot, and see if kitty claims that area as her own. You might also try getting your cat a pet bed to ensure sweet dreams for all. Place it on the floor next to your bed so that she can be close to you without being on top of you. Make sure you've handled the new bed so it has your scent on it. You could also try a cozy piece of fleece, which most cats love, or a small carpeted tree house placed in the corner of the room.

Aggressively playful cats should be kept out of the bedroom, or you'll get no sleep at all. If you don't want your cat to feel left out, try to nap with him at another time during the day. That way, you'll be able to cuddle together for a while and still get the rest you need. Another strategy is to engage your cat in some pre-bedtime play that allows him to run, chase, pounce, climb, and jump. This will burn up some of that late-night kitty energy so that he is ready to settle down when you are.

If your kitty has an early morning alarm clock that says "breakfast time" and impels her to knock things over, climb over your face, knead the blankets, and generally make a lot of noise, you might try an automatic food dispenser, which is set to a timer. Available in most pet stores and online, these handy devices will serve breakfast while you snooze.

DISTINCTIVE FELINE
SALLY—CLOSE ENCOUNTERS

Sally is a perfectly normal feline in every way—except when she is in the grip of some psychic event that only she can see. There must be invisible inhabitants of the apartment where she lives, because Sally will be calm one minute, and then leap up and run into another room, staring at something which is not supposed to be there. The first time it happened, it really gave me the creeps. She shot up from her chair, ran over to the wall, and watched something climb the wall, slide across the ceiling, and down the opposite wall. Since Sally is not scared during these events—there is no hissing or menacing behavior—whatever is there is not threatening. Not yet, anyway.

Lessons from Sally

If you like the paranormal, a psychic kitty is for you. If not, then know that cats are very sensitive to their environment, seen and unseen. They are also sensitive to you and your emotions, so enjoy sharing a psychic connection and some quality time.

PULLING A DISAPPEARING ACT

Why is it that our cats pick the worst times, like when we are leaving for work, to pull a disappearing act? And they find such good hiding places! At times it seems the more you look for them, the more they dig in. Sometimes on a house call, I will sit quietly waiting for missing cats to reappear. When they do, I am usually greeted by a "deer in the headlights" stare, but at least I know they are in the house.

One kitty, Percy, was so shy that no amount of time or trouble would bring him into the open. This is where a cat sitter needs to be creative. To make sure that he was alive and well, I sprinkled oatmeal flakes around his food bowls and, sure enough, when I returned later, there were Percy's paw prints.

If one of your cats has gone AWOL, check all of the out-of-sight places such as the area under the bed, crawl spaces, gaps behind furniture, and dresser drawers. You might also inspect your box spring. If there is hole in it, your cat might be snoozing in there. Also examine washing machines and dryers. I had a client whose cat, Katie, jumped into a warm dryer after the clothes were taken out. Thank goodness she was discovered before another load was put in.

You can also use food to lure a missing kitty out of hiding. Open the refrigerator door, pop a can of food, or shake a bag of treats—anything that she associates with mealtime. Chances are, she will appear to claim her reward.

Hiding is a natural instinct for cats, because they like to know that they will be safe from predators when they sleep. It's important to provide acceptable hiding places such as a cat tree with cubby holes, a closet you don't mind leaving open all day (with something to keep the door from slamming shut), or a cardboard box. A hiding place that you choose will make your cat feel more secure and allow you to find him without a frantic search.

All cats love hiding places. To prevent your cat from disappearing to parts unknown, try to create cozy hiding spaces just for her. A cat tree with cubby holes, an open closet, or even a cardboard box can often fill the bill.

Milly Carves Herself a Nest

Scratching is a natural part of a cat's life, but some take it to extremes. I remember Milly, one of my house calls, who scratched a hole in her owner's box spring big enough to crawl into and take a snooze. Fortunately, Milly's owners told me about her special spot before I came in to care for her. Never in a million years would I have thought to look for her there, and I've seen some pretty exotic hiding places.

PLAYING ROUGH

It's important to teach kittens that fingers, toes, and other body parts are not playthings. For this reason, it's best not to play games in which you move your hand under a blanket, pretending to be prey, or to encourage cats to pounce on or swat you. This might be cute when they're kittens, but it's not fun when they're adult cats and can draw blood.

If your kitten or adult cat starts biting you, immediately stop petting him and ignore him for a few seconds. *Never* hit your cat, because he will not associate the punishment with his inappropriate behavior. Instead, redirect kitty's attention to a toy. Reward him for playing with his toys with praise or treats, and he'll soon learn that hands are for petting and toys are for playing.

Fritz Gets Feisty

One of my clients has a cat named Fritz who is wonderful and loving with her—but unfriendly to everyone else. Once I open the door, he begins lunging at my feet as I sidestep my way into the kitchen. I know Fritz is not trying to hurt me; I think he is just afraid and defending his space. Fortunately, as soon as I put his food bowl down, he is much more interested in that than me, so it all works out.

ACTING AGGRESSIVE TOWARD PEOPLE OR OTHER PETS

Never hit your cat. He will not understand the punishment, and you may do lasting damage to your relationship. Love and patience are the best cat-training tools.

If your cat was aggressive when you got him, he might have experienced some type of trauma or abuse, and his trust will need to be earned with a great deal of love and patience. You and your cat might benefit from the counsel and recommendations of a feline behaviorist.

If your normally friendly cat starts acting aggressively toward you or toward other household pets, talk to your veterinarian, because it could be a sign your cat isn't feeling well. Headaches, hypertension, and hyperthyroidism can all trigger aggression.

Once a medical condition is ruled out, you can consult a feline behaviorist about the environmental changes that might have triggered the aggression, such as a new person or pet in your household, the absence of a family member, a move, or a neighborhood cat that hangs out on your patio. If possible, modify the environment so that things go back to "normal." If this cannot be done, it will take time for your cat to adjust, but take heart, because cats can adapt to new things in time. During the transition, you might try a pheromone product, which can calm an anxious cat by simulating feline facial pheromones. These products are available in pet stores as plug-ins, sprays, and collars.

Holistic veterinarians swear by flower essences for treating fear, aggression, and other stress-related problems. Always use a formulation that is made specifically for cats, so you don't overdose your cat with a product intended for humans or other animals. Also use one that is alcohol-free, as cats are sensitive to alcohol. In extreme cases, veterinarians can prescribe tranquilizers.

Kindness and patience are the best tools for training your cat. If you can help him associate objectionable behaviors with unpleasant deterrents and wanted actions with treats, toys, and affection, your kitty will soon get the picture and choose desirable behavior. This, in turn, will result in a happy, healthy cat who respects both you and your home.

Playtime and
Special Occasions

Cats love to play, and it is very important for their overall health and well-being. I make sure to play with my own cats every day and do the same with those I care for as a sitter. Toys and games are wonderful for your kitty and a great deal of fun for you, as well. Who can resist a kitten scampering across the floor in hot pursuit of a toy mouse or a cat leaping to catch a prize that's been tossed in the air?

When I make my house calls, I always carry a backpack loaded with the essentials, including toys and catnip. Most of the cats in my charge love catnip—sometimes too much. During one visit, I dropped my pack on a chair in the living room and went into the kitchen to prepare food for Feather, a tabby, and Necktie, a tortoiseshell. I didn't real-

Feline Fact
Whether at play
or escaping from
danger, a domestic cat
can sprint at about
thirty miles per hour.

ize that I had forgotten to zip the pack shut. When I finished working in the kitchen, I found that the cats had dragged my backpack off the chair. They had rooted through the contents—drooling on most of the items, including my wallet—and tossed everything all over the floor in order to find the prized catnip.

Fortunately, I kept my cache sealed in a container, so that Feather and Necktie couldn't get into it and scatter it everywhere. I could only laugh because it was my own fault. Meanwhile, I figured they had truly earned a reward for all their efforts, so I gave them each some of the dried leaves. Now I always check the zipper and hang my backpack on a doorknob.

Certain toys and household items are dangerous to your kitty if you are not around to supervise him during play. That's why this chapter offers not only suggestions for toys and activities, but also playtime safety tips. Since the holidays, too, can be both fun and potentially hazardous, safety pointers are included for special occasions, as well. With some care, you can make every day, including holidays, both safe and fun for you and your kitty.

PLAYTIME IS KEY

I've never known a cat who did not like to play. It is part of feline makeup and something we can easily share with our furry friends. In addition, it helps our cats in all sorts of wonderful ways. Playtime provides your kitty with the exercise she needs to keep her slim and trim, and gives her an outlet for any pent-up energy—and we all know how energetic cats can be, especially kittens. Also, when you share interac-

Play is important for a
cat's general health and
well-being. It provides
valuable muscle-toning
exercise, controls
weight, and gives kitty
an outlet for any
pent-up energy.

tive play with your kitty, it becomes a positive bonding experience for the both of you.

Cats also need to play to keep from becoming bored. A bored cat might eat to pass the time and grow overweight, much like a bored human. A feline who's bored might also get into mischief around your house. Cats need mental stimulation just as people do.

Toys, Treats, and Activities

You can make a fun cat toy out of the most basic household items like tissue paper, a box, or a pipe cleaner. I always say that the simplest toys are the best. Make your own catnip toy by stuffing some of the dried herb into an old sock or a small cloth and knotting it shut. Wedge that into a cardboard toilet paper roll, and you have the perfect interactive toy. Shopping bags are fun, too, but be sure to cut off the handles before you offer the bag to your kitty. (See the inset on page 105 for more about shopping bag safety.)

If your kitty loves to chase things—and what kitty doesn't?—try rolling a piece of aluminum foil into a large ball to keep her on the run.

Interactive play, in which you share an activity with your cat, provides all the benefits of solo play while also helping you and your kitty bond.

Martha Says "No" to Catnip

I once had a client who sprinkled dry catnip on everything, including her cat Martha's food, the poor girl. For this cat, it would have been a treat *not* to have any catnip. I told my client that catnip should be given occasionally, once or twice a week, but never in food as it may upset eating habits.

Feline Fact

About 80 percent of cats are attracted to the mint known as catnip (*Nepeta cataria*) and respond by rolling on the floor, dashing around the house, or becoming mellow and sleepy. Researchers don't know for sure how catnip works its magic, but they suspect it mimics feline "happy" pheromones.

To revive store-bought catnip-stuffed toys that have lost their zing, submerge the toy in hot water and then immediately squeeze the water out. When the toy is dry, the catnip will be more aromatic.

Cats also love to chase the light of a flashlight or penlight, but be careful with laser pet toys. You never want to point a laser toward your cat's face or eyes.

There are many great toys to be found in pet stores, as well. Look for a long, springy wire with bits of cardboard attached to the end, or the circular plastic track that encloses a ball and has a corrugated cardboard center for scratching. Fishing pole toys are another wonderful idea and perfect for interactive play.

Catnip is a winner in my household. Most, but not all, cats enjoy this dried herb, which I have found to be perfectly safe and fun. Its scent attracts most cats, and mine really love to roll in it. Besides making simple toys out of it, you can use it to stimulate your cat's interest in using scratching posts. Sprinkle it on, rubbing it a bit as you do to release the scent. It is also good to put a little of the herb in a cat carrier when it's time to go to the vet's office. In between uses, store the container of dried catnip in the refrigerator to help it last a little longer. Be on the alert when your cat has been enjoying a roll in the catnip because he might play more aggressively. Other than that, enjoy the fun—your kitty will.

If you have invested in commercial catnip-stuffed toys, you know that they are usually not as potent as separately sold dry catnip, and tend to lose their zing quickly. One trick for increasing the longevity of catnip toys is to put them under hot water, then squeeze the water out. It rejuvenates the catnip and saves you the cost of buying new toys. To prevent boredom, I suggest that you always leave a few toys out for play while keeping the rest out of sight. Rotate the toys frequently so that your cat always has something new to pique her interest.

Basic Safety Tips for Cat Toys

As fun and important as cat toys can be, they can also prove hazardous when you're not around to supervise kitty's play. The following guidelines will help you keep your cat safe.

- ✿ When you're finished playing with interactive toys such as fishing poles, ribbons, and strings, put them away where your cat can't get to them. You don't want kitty chewing on, swallowing, or getting caught up in the fishing line or string.

When you're finished using a cat fishing pole or any other toy that includes a string, strip of cloth, or feathers, store it out of kitty's reach. You don't want your cat chewing, swallowing, or getting tangled in the toy.

PAPER SHOPPING BAGS

Although you may never have thought about this, paper shopping bags can be a danger to your kitties. Let me tell you about Moon and Jet, two cute charcoal-gray sisters I cared for one Christmas. As soon as I arrived in their apartment that cold winter's day, I knew something awful had happened. The place was in chaos, with objects overturned and strewn all over the floor. Jet was visible, but I could not find Moon. Finally, I heard a pitiful mewing under the bed and there she was, huddled with a shopping bag handle wrapped around her neck and under her leg. It was a wonder she could breathe.

Cats love playing with bags, but she had obviously gotten her head entangled in the handle and, in an effort to remove it, had caught her paw in it as well. The chaos in the house was the result of her frenzied attempts to free herself from what could have been a noose. Moon was completely exhausted, so she put up no resistance when I gently pulled her out from under the bed. The handle was wrapped so tightly, I had to use nail scissors to cut through it. I was so happy when this usually shy kitty let me cuddle her and make sure that she was okay.

Please cut the handles off of any shopping bags within your cats' reach. Since that experience with Moon, I have not been shy about doing this myself during my house calls.

Piglet Takes a Bath

One of my long-term cat-sitting charges, Piglet, piles her toys in her water bowl and makes a complete mess when trying to get them out. Her owners have learned to live with this behavior and now keep her water bowls in the bathtub!

🐾 Don't leave any toys with feathers out for your kitty when you are not there. Swallowing feathers is dangerous.

🐾 Watch out for plush toys, as cats can rip them open and pull out the stuffing, which can be harmful if ingested. I prefer toys that are filled with 100-percent catnip.

For safety, choose 100-percent catnip-filled toys over stuffing-filled products. The stuffing can be harmful if your cat rips the toy open and swallows it.

🐾 Keep your scratching post in good shape. If it's covered with carpeting, tiny threads can come loose with use. Cut these threads off with a scissor before your cat swallows them, or better yet, provide a scratching post that's covered with sisal instead of carpet.

🐾 Always check floors and other surfaces for household items like dropped pins, needles, paper clips, rubber bands, dental floss, or pills. Although kitty may enjoy batting these things around, they pose a real hazard.

Playtime is fun time for cats of all ages. Younger cats require more active play, but older cats still want to engage, although they might prefer that you do most of the work. When you get pooped, put on one of the specially designed cat videos that show fast-moving scenes of birds, bees, and small animals—perfect kitty entertainment. Or you might try a battery-operated toy. The bottom line is to make time for playtime in your schedule. Your cats will love you for it.

When you're too pooped to play, try a specially designed cat video or a battery-operated toy.

HAPPY HOLIDAYS FOR ALL

Holidays are a time to enjoy yourself, and there is no reason why your cats can't enjoy them too—provided you take some precautions.

I remember a client who loved to throw wild New Year's Eve parties with lots of food and drink. One year, she threw her festive party

Christmas trees
can pose a danger
to inquisitive cats.
Avoid putting
chemicals in the water;
use garlands instead
of tinsel, which can
be swallowed; and
keep ornament
hooks and ribbons
away from kitty.

and left the next day for a vacation. As always, I came in to care for her two cats, Boo and Bella. When I entered the apartment, I found the kitchen in an uproar! The floor was littered with plastic cups, straws, napkins, streamers, wine corks, bits of cheese, olive pits, and other food. The garbage had been bagged and sealed but left in the kitchen, where Boo and Bella had helped themselves to an "after" party. Thank goodness they didn't eat anything harmful, but they obviously enjoyed the wine corks; I found them all over the house.

Holidays are fun for all of us, but crowded parties and high-decibel festivities can be stressful for your cat, and certain foods and decorations can prove hazardous. I want to share some commonsense precautions to ensure that your feline friend enjoys many special occasions along with you.

Keeping Kitty Safe From Decorations

If you have a live Christmas tree, please make sure it is securely anchored, and do not put chemicals in the tree water. I suggest keeping

Murray's Holiday Treat

Christmas tree tinsel and kitties do not mix. I remember Murray, a sweet-natured black and white kitty, who greeted me one December evening during a house call with several inches of tinsel hanging out of his rear end! Afraid that he might lick the tinsel and swallow it again, I very gently removed it from his behind. Fortunately, he was a good sport.

the water bowl covered with a tree skirt so cats won't be tempted to drink it. Keep pine needles off the floor, and poisonous plants such as mistletoe and poinsettias out of reach. Use garlands instead of tinsel to decorate the tree. If swallowed, tinsel can get caught in the intestines and cause major medical problems. The same is true of the silk thread that is wrapped around some ornaments. While hanging ornaments, be careful not to drop the small hooks, which could be real trouble if swallowed or chewed.

In addition to tinsel, do not let your cat play with the thin ribbons used to decorate gifts. If swallowed, they could become lodged in the intestines and cause life-threatening obstructions. After opening your gifts, used wrapping paper is always a fun plaything for cats, but not packing material such as small Styrofoam pellets. Always dispose of that immediately.

Candles are festive at any time of year, but please don't leave lit candles unattended where your cat can reach them. It takes a curious kitty just a few seconds to get too close to a flame and wind up with burnt whiskers or something far worse.

If kitty wants to share in the fun of gift wrapping, let him play with wrapping or tissue paper, but make sure he doesn't eat it. Ribbons and Styrofoam packing pellets can be swallowed, so keep them away from your cat.

Keeping Kitty Safe During Holiday Parties

Whenever you have a party in your house, it is best to keep your cats in a separate room behind closed doors with their food, water, litter, toys, and treats. I even put a "Do Not Disturb" sign on the door of the room I designate as theirs when entertaining. Large crowds and a lot of noise can scare cats, and you do not want them running out an open door, God forbid.

Halloween Kitty

Instead of trying to dress up your kitty for Halloween—which many cats, quite naturally, would object to—dress your child up as the family cat. Take a close-up picture of your cat's face, enlarge it on the computer, print it out on heavyweight paper, and make a simple mask. Add a fake tail and leopard pajamas, and you will have both a fun family project and a winning trick-or-treat outfit.

During party prep, keep your cats out of the kitchen and out of mischief. You don't want them jumping up onto hot stoves. People food is off-limits at any time of year, except under unusual circumstances and with your vet's permission, so please make sure that no guest tries to get your cats in the holiday mood with a bit of spirits or chocolate—both can make them sick. In fact, never allow guests to give your kitties *any* people food or drink.

If you're planning a big party, designate a special room where your cat can feel safe and secure behind closed doors. Furnish the room with food, water, a litter box, and toys, and place a "Do Not Disturb" sign on the door.

Once everyone goes home, check the floors for any dropped food, glasses, wine corks, toothpicks, etc. All of these items can be harmful, as can tobacco, so clean out the ashtrays too. Please bag all garbage, and if you cannot put it outside, secure it in a place where your cat cannot reach it.

I once knew a cat named Ginny who got into an open garbage pail in the middle of the night and ended up with her head stuck in a tin can. She ran around the house in a panic, banging the walls to try to dislodge the can—which only wedged her head in more tightly. If her owner hadn't awakened from all the noise, it might have been a real

DISTINCTIVE FELINE
ELOISE—
THE ULTIMATE COUCH POTATO

Eloise was fortunate enough to have owners who were delighted to play with her, but her favorite pastime was to watch television—after finding the remote control and selecting a channel, that is. A gigantic flat-screen TV was mounted on the wall of her owners' master bedroom, and Eloise would turn the television on, make herself comfortable on the bed, and settle in for hours of happy viewing. On my first cat-sitting visit, I was startled to hear the television on in the bedroom. Thinking that the owners had simply forgotten to turn the set off before they left for vacation, I turned it off for them. The next day, I found Eloise on the bed with the television on again! Shaken, I called the owners, who confirmed that Eloise turned the TV on all the time, adding that she was particularly fond of sports channels.

Lessons from Eloise

There is no limit to the curiosity and ingenuity of the feline. Just when you think that you have cats all figured out, they do something that takes you by surprise. I am a firm believer that they are much more aware of our world than we think they are; they simply pay attention only to what interests them and ignore the rest. Encourage their inquisitiveness in a safe way.

During the holiday season, set aside quality time to spend with your cat so that he doesn't feel neglected.

tragedy. Thankfully, it wasn't. Ginny learned her lesson and gave the garbage pail a wide berth from then on.

With the proper preparation, the holidays can be fun for your entire household, including your cats. In fact, since you know that cats love to play, this is an excellent time of year to replenish your collection of feline toys and treats. With all the hustle and bustle of the season, I make sure to spend extra quality time with my kitties each day so they don't feel left out.

The smallest amount of care and affection we show our wonderful feline friends is given back to us tenfold. We need to be sure that playtime makes our kitties happy and keeps them safe, particularly during the holidays. I wish you and yours the very best all year round.

Conclusion

Now you know that my life as a cat sitter is very rewarding and never dull. I have enjoyed telling my stories and sharing my "commonsense" cat care advice with you, and *Cat Fancy* editor Susan Logan has been the perfect person to help me do it.

Perhaps my tales have inspired you to think about trying cat sitting as a profession. If so, let me make sure you have all the facts.

I have met many wonderful and caring people and their wonderful cats, but anyone who wants to pursue this has to know that you need to be available to work seven days a week, and your busiest times are weekends and holidays. You will be working when other people are away on vacation or enjoying the holidays with friends and family. When I started, there was no one else in Manhattan doing full-time in-home cat sitting. Now, it's a very competitive business. To build and keep a loyal clientele, you must be available 24/7.

Responsibility is key. You must travel to your clients' homes and take care of their cats no matter what. That includes trudging through snowstorms, torrential rains, heat waves, and more. Also, if you don't see the cats you are caring for in the home, you have to make sure they are there—no matter what it takes. I found one poor kitty who had gotten himself locked in a closet in the owner's rush to leave, and another, in a dresser drawer.

Not all cats you care for will be friendly, but most will be happy for some TLC and to have their needs taken care of.

The bottom line is that I love what I do, and the satisfaction I get out of this unusual line of work far outweighs any sacrifices I have made along the way. I look forward to each day and to seeing the wonderful kitties I care for.

Because of our love of cats, Susan Logan and I are great believers in supporting local animal shelters, rescue organizations, and animal charities, and we urge you to do the same. Just a small donation can make a huge difference in a cat's life. Or, you might consider volunteering.

Susan joins me in wishing you and the cats you love the very best.

About the Authors

Jeanne Adlon has been deeply involved with animals for over thirty-five years. Although she trained as a fine artist with hopes of being a fashion designer, fate took another turn when she met celebrated author and critic Cleveland Amory, and started working for his Fund for Animals organization in 1970. She even cared for his beloved cat Polar Bear, made famous in *The Cat Who Came for Christmas*. Four years later, she opened Cat Cottage, the first store in Manhattan created specifically for cats and cat lovers, and went on to become the city's first full-time cat sitter. Jeanne has devoted her life and career to the care of other people's cats, and has watched over hundreds of our feline friends. In between house calls, she writes a popular weekly column as a Cat Expert on www.CatChannel.com. She shares her home with several rescued cats and a perky little pooch named Ziggy.

Susan Logan, a lifelong animal lover, is the editor of *Cat Fancy* magazine, the premiere publication in its field. Published by BowTie, Inc., *Cat Fancy* is the world's most widely read cat care and lifestyle magazine. With more than twenty years of journalism experience, Susan has spent the last ten years devoted to pet and veterinary subjects at BowTie and is a regular speaker at the Cat Writers' Association. In 2006 and 2007, she was awarded the Muse Medallion, the association's highest honor, for her insightful series of editorials in *Cat Fancy.* In 2010, she was awarded the Winn Feline Foundation's media appreciation award. Susan is the proud parent of Maine Coon mixes, Madison and Sophie. When she isn't writing and editing, she enjoys singing, running, and hanging out with her two-legged and four-legged family and friends.

Index